INSIGHT GUIDES

PRAGUE
smart guide

Areas

Contents

A–Z

Below: the Spanish
Synagogue.

Left: bridges across the Vltava.

Atlas

Below: sculpture at the Strahov Monastery.

Prague

L ocated at the heart of Europe, Prague ('Praha' in Czech) has been the capital of the ancient realm of Bohemia for centuries. It has been a capital for the Holy Roman Empire, the Habsburg Court and the state of Czechoslovakia. It was only when the Iron Curtain fell in 1989 that Prague's cultural treasures – miraculously preserved – were unveiled once more.

The Five Towns

Prague used to be known as the 'Five Towns', and although it has now been divided into 10 separate districts, most visitors concentrate on the five historic towns: Hradčany, Staré Město (Old Town), Malá Strana (Lesser Quarter), Nové Město (New Town) and the the Jewish Quarter. In earlier times, the inhabitants of the congested Old Town and Josefov, the old Jewish Quarter, must have felt envious when they looked across to the New Town, where the far-sighted designs of Charles IV (1346–78) and his architects had created broad, open spaces and avenues such as the Charles and Wenceslas squares. Today, however, the Old Town has been beautifully restored, and Josefov's Paěížská is a chic avenue lined with expensive shops.

The City's Growth

As the city expanded, further districts were added to the original five towns. The incorporation of Vyšehrad, Holešovice and Bubeneč brought the population to around 200,000 by 1900. After World War I, the city's area tripled to a size of 550 sq km (190 sq miles), and by 1930 the population had reached 850,000. Under communism new suburbs were built, and the southwestern suburb of Jihozápadní Město is a site of ongoing expansion. Today, the city has a population of around 1.2 million, while its wider metropolitan area is estimated to accommodate over 1.9 million people.

The Vltava River

As Prague's architecture envelops you, you could be forgiven for overlooking one of the city's most beautiful sights: the Vltava River, its graceful S-shape unwinding in the heart of the city. A tributary of the Elbe, and at times going under its German name of Moldau, it has inspired writers and musicians alike, notably Bedřich Smetana, whose symphonic poems celebrate its journey across the Czech landscape on its way to Prague.

Getting Around

Prague's public transport infrastructure is very good and consists of an integrated transport system with the metro, a tram, buses, the Petřín funicular and three ferries. All services

Below: view from Prague Castle.

have a common ticketing system, and, in comparison with public transport in other European cities, prices are surprisingly inexpensive.

Life Since the Velvet Revolution

Since 1989, there have been many changes for both the city and its people. Although the optimism that followed the Velvet Revolution has now died down – not least as the Czechs face up to life under capitalism, membership of the EU and NATO – there is still a sense that the city is rediscovering and reinventing its past.

Some complain that city life now seems beholden to materialism. Prague's days as a centre of writers and artists have nearly vanished, along with the idealism of intellectual life under the tyranny of communism.

There are, however, benefits to the embracing of capitalist economics. Prague has prospered in recent years. It hosts the European headquarters of many international companies, and its manufacturing industries – including textiles, engineering and brewing – have survived the transition to the free market. Furthermore, the city's architectural heritage has brought a new industry that dwarfs the old, as an estimated 60 percent of the city's income now derives from tourism. This in turn has allowed historic buildings to benefit from a massive renovation programme and important new buildings to be commissioned from the likes of Frank Gehry and Jean Nouvel.

Highlights

▲ The world's largest **castle** contains St Vitus Cathedral, the Old Royal Palace and numerous chapels, galleries and gardens.
▶ Visit Prague's pubs for arguably the world's finest **beer** or tour the Staropramen Brewery.

▶ With its synagogues, cemetery and cobbled streets, the **Jewish Quarter** is the world of Kafka, Rabbi Löw and the Golem.

▲ Prague's iconic **Charles Bridge** is lined with fine Baroque statues, each with a story to tell.

▲ **Strahov Monastery** contains two exquisite Baroque libraries.
▶ Wonderfully preserved medieval, Baroque and Rococo buildings frame **Old Town Square**.

Malá Strana

Occupying the slopes between the river and the castle, Malá Strana, or 'Lesser Quarter', constitutes the most intact Baroque townscape in Central Europe. From humble 9th-century beginnings, it grew in the 13th century when German merchants arrived. During the reign of Charles IV (1346–78) it experienced a boom, only to suffer major damage in the Hussite Wars, and then in the Great Fire of 1541. The district blossomed again after the Thirty Years War, when the redistribution of property to Habsburg supporters initiated a building frenzy. Although the court moved back to Vienna, its palaces and merchants' houses have remained intact to this day.

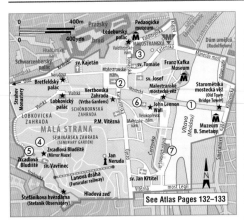

See Atlas Pages 132–133

In the middle of the square is the **Church of St Nicholas** ②, probably Prague's finest Baroque building and a potent symbol of the Counter-Reformation. It was begun in the early 18th century by Bavarian architect Christoph Dientzenhofer, continued by his son, Kilián Ignaz, and completed by Anselmo Lurago in 1755. The recently restored interior has one of the largest ceiling frescoes in Europe, painted by Johann Lukas Kracker in 1770.
SEE ALSO CHURCHES, P.42

Charles Bridge

The **Charles Bridge** ① was commissioned by Charles IV in 1357, built by Petr Parléř (who also designed St Vitus's Cathedral), and completed in about 1400. It has withstood centuries of traffic and numerous floods, thanks, so legend has it, to the use of eggs in the mortar.

Crossing the bridge itself, you pass several statues and monuments, most of which are copies of the Baroque originals.
SEE ALSO MONUMENTS, P.78

Lesser Town Square

Following **Mostecká** (Bridge Street) from the Charles Bridge into Malá Strana, you soon come to the **Malostranské náměstí** (Lesser Town Square), lined with the palaces of the nobility.

The Wallenstein Palace and Gardens

To the north of Malostranské náměstí, down Tomašská and Valdštejnská is the **Wallenstein Palace and Gardens** ③. The first Baroque palace in Prague, it was built between 1624 and 1630 for General Albrecht von Wallenstein (1583–1634), who had done rather well out of the Thirty Years War.

Today, its frescoed interior is home to the Czech Senate, although various rooms are also open to the public. The magnificent gardens – with their grotto, ponds and aviary – are overlooked by a triple-

Left: Wallenstein Palace.

Left: crowds filling the narrow streets near Charles Bridge.

sunspots; on clear nights it looks out at the moon, stars and planets.
SEE ALSO CHILDREN, P.40, 41; MONUMENTS, P.80; PARKS AND GARDENS, P.108

Maltese Square

A little further towards the river, you come to the **Maltézské náměstí** (Maltese Square). Its name derives from the fact that the Knights of Malta founded a monastery here in 1169, just behind where the Gothic **Church of Our Lady Beneath the Chain** ⑥ stands to this day. Continuing towards the river, you pass the **John Lennon Wall**, which is strewn with graffiti in homage to The Beatles.
SEE ALSO CHURCHES, P.42; MONUMENTS, P.79

Kampa Park

Alongside the river is **Kampa Park**, a green space formed in 1940 by linking up the gardens of former palaces. In a converted watermill on the riverbanks themselves is the **Kampa Gallery** ⑦. Based around the collections of wealthy Czech ex-pats Jan and Meda Mladek, the museum displays contemporary Central European art.
SEE ALSO MUSEUMS AND GALLERIES, P.82

arched loggia where Wallenstein dined during the 12 months he lived in the palace.
SEE ALSO CASTLES, PALACES AND HOUSES, P.34; PARKS AND GARDENS, P.108

Nerudova

Back at Malostranské náměstí, heading west up the hill towards the castle is the street of Nerudova, named after the Czech poet and author Jan Neruda (1834–91), who lived at no. 47, and whose work *Tales of the Lesser Quarter* was inspired by the everyday life of Malá Strana.

Many of the houses on Nerudova have house signs, which date from the time before house numbers were introduced (in 1770 by Josef II). The Three Violins (several generations of violin-makers lived here) is at no. 12, The Golden Chalice is at no. 16 and The Donkey and the Cradle is at no. 25.

Petřín Hill

The southern part of Malá Strana is dominated by **Petřín Hill** ④, an area that was once occupied by vineyards and a quarry, and is now a large park. Many visitors will ascend the hill by the funicular railway on its eastern slopes. Others may choose to access the park via the Strahov Monastery in Hradčany *(see p.9)*. Part of the park – known as the **Seminary Garden** – is still maintained by the monks as an orchard.

On the crest of the hill is the **Observation Tower** ⑤, a replica of the Eiffel Tower that offers great views of the city.

Close by is the **Mirror Maze**, a mock-Gothic castle popular with children and containing a hall of distorting mirrors.

Just over the brow of the hill is the **Stefanik Observatory**. During the day, its 1928 Zeiss telescope is trained on Mercury and Venus as well as

At the bottom of Petřín Hill, just to the south of Malostranské náměstí are the **Vrtba Gardens**. This World Heritage Site offers perhaps the finest example of Baroque landscaping in Prague. The gardens also contain a number of sculptures by Matthias Bernhard Braun and a pavilion with frescoes by Václav Vavřinec Reiner. *See also Parks and Gardens, p.108.*

Hradčany

Dominating the hill on the left bank of the Vltava is Prague's castle district, Hradčany. The history of the city begins with the construction of the castle in the 9th century. Its attractive mix of palaces, churches, museums, gardens and galleries provides a fascinating insight into the history of Prague. Beyond the boundary of the castle proper are some of the most charming streets in the city, palaces containing major collections of the National Gallery and Prague's most important pilgrimage site, as well as the magnificent Strahov Monastery site with its ornate Baroque libraries and art collection.

Prague Castle

Prague Castle, or Pražský hrad, sprawls across the district known as Hradčany. More than 1,000 years old, it was the residence of the early Přemyslid rulers, who did well to establish their headquarters in this strategic position over the Vltava. Generations of rulers continued to expand the complex with churches and palaces, defensive and residential buildings.

It is also the spiritual centre of the city as site of the Cathedral of St Vitus, and it retains its link with temporal power as the residence of the president of the Czech Republic.

CASTLE SIGHTS

At the far eastern end of the castle are the Old Castle Steps. Ascending these from Malostranská metro brings you to the **Black Tower** (*Černá věž*), entrance to the castle proper. On the left is the entrance to the gardens on the castle's southern ramparts, which lead down to Malá Strana below.

Passing through the gate on the left is the entrance to the **Lobkowicz Palace**, while further up Jiřská and to the right is the entrance to the attractive **Zlatá ulička** (Golden Lane), one of the most popular – and crowded – attractions of the castle. At the end of the lane is the **Dalibor Tower** (*Daliborka*), part of the castle wall.

Jiřská ends at **Náměstí sv. Jiří** (St George's Square). Immediately on the right is the **Basilica of St George** ① (*Bazilika sv. Jiří*), the oldest church still standing in the castle complex. The church

Left: detail from St Vitus's Cathedral. **Far left:** inside the Strahov Monastery.

right is the Rococo **Archbishop's Palace**, behind which in the **Sternberg Palace** ⑤ is the collection of European painting from the Classical era to the end of the Baroque of the National Gallery. Opposite, in the Renaissance sgraffitoed **Schwarzenberg Palace** is another branch of the National Gallery containing Baroque art in Bohemia. SEE ALSO MUSEUMS AND GALLERIES, P.84

The Loreta and Strahov

Continuing west from Hradčanské náměstí brings you to Loretánské náměstí. On the left-hand-side of the square is the façade of the **Černín Palace** and opposite is one of Prague's most important religious complexes, the **Loreta** ⑥. Just below Loretánské náměstí (at the end of Kapuchínská) is **Nový svět**, a tiny row of houses that is one of the most attractive in Hradčany.

At the far end of Loretánská, just beyond where it joins Úvoz, is the **Strahov Monastery** ⑦, the oldest monastery in Bohemia founded by the Premonstratensians in 1140. SEE ALSO CASTLES, PALACES AND HOUSES, P.34; CHURCHES, P.44, 46; MUSEUMS AND GALLERIES, P.86

was once part of a large monastic complex.

Dominating Námestí sv. Jiří is the large bulk of **St Vitus's Cathedral** ② *(Katedrála sv. Víta)*, the entrance to which is further on at its western end. The cathedral is the largest church in Prague, the metropolitan church of the Archdiocese of Prague, the royal and imperial burial church and also the place where the royal regalia are kept.

Just to the south of the cathedral in the castle's Third Coutyard is the entrance to the **Old Royal Palace** *(Starý královský palác)*. Below the palace is the **Story of Prague Castle**, an exhibition that provides an excellent introduction to the castle's history. Also in the Third Courtyard is the Gothic **Equestrian Statue of St George**.

Carrying on from the western front of the cathedral takes you into the Second Courtyard, where the **Prague Castle Picture Gallery** ③ *(Obrazárna Pražského hradu)* is located. SEE ALSO CASTLES, PALACES AND HOUSES, P.35–7; CHURCHES, P.43, 44; MUSEUMS AND GALLERIES, P.83

The Castle Gardens

Across the U Prasného most (bridge) heading north from the Third Courtyard are the **Royal Gardens** *(Královská zahrada)*. These are home to two important Renaissance buildings. The first is the **Ball-Game Court** *(Míčovna)*, the second is the **Summer Palace** ④ *(Belvedér)*. SEE ALSO PARKS AND GARDENS, P.109

Hradčanské Náměstí

Beyond the Third Courtyard is the **Matthias Gate** *(Matyášova brána)* that leads out into the spacious **Hradčanské náměstí** (Hradčany Square). On the

The Dalibor Tower is the setting for Smetana's nationalist opera *Dalibor*, inspired by the imprisonment of Duke Dalibor in the tower during the 15th century. According to legend, the music he made while locked up was so exquisite it attracted crowds of people to the foot of the tower to listen.

Staré Město

Staré Město or 'Old Town' is located on the east bank of the Vltava. Its network of narrow streets and unexpected squares – lined with palaces, theatres and museums – tell of a history of prosperous trade and civic culture. But the district was also forged by religious differences. Its churches, monastic houses and university buildings are the legacies of the Reformation and Counter-Reformation, while the district's northern section forms the Jewish Quarter, which retains its historic synagogues and cemetery. It is all marvellously preserved, and while the main architectural style is Baroque, there are also medieval, Rococo, neo-Renaissance and Art Nouveau buildings to enjoy.

The Royal Way

Weaving through Staré Město is the Royal Way – the processional route followed by Czech kings on their way to be crowned in St Vitus's Cathedral in Hradčany *(see p.9)*. It begins at the Gothic **Powder Gate** ① *(Prašna brána)* at the eastern end of Staré Město and proceeds along Celetná, through Old Town Square, along Karlova and across the Charles Bridge to Malá Strana, where it climbs up Nerudova to the castle.

Important sights can be seen along the route, including the extravagant Art Nouveau **Municipal House** *(Obecní dům)*, the Cubist **House of the Black Madonna** *(Dům u Černé Matky boží)*, the Astronomical Clock and the Clementinum, before reaching the Charles Bridge.

SEE ALSO ARCHITECTURE, P.28; MUSEUMS AND GALLERIES, P.87

Originally the Old Town lay 2–3m (6–9ft) below the modern street level. The area, however, was vulnerable to flooding; consequently the street level has been gradually raised since the late 13th century. Many of the district's houses still have Romanesque rooms hidden in their basements.

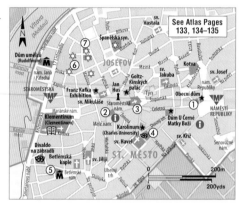

See Atlas Pages 133, 134–135

Old Town Square

Dominating the west side of the Old Town Square *(Staroměstské náměstí)* is the **Old Town Hall** ② *(Staroměstské radnice)*. Founded in 1338, it was put together from a collection of medieval buildings, purchased one by one over the years with the proceeds of the city's tax on wine. Today you can visit the 15th-century council chamber, the chapel, the dungeons and the tower. On the side of the town hall (facing Little Square – *Malé náměstí*) is the **Astronomical Clock**, which attracts crowds to watch the mechanical figures strike the hour.

In the middle of Old Town Square is the **memorial** to the Protestant reformer Jan Hus, erected on the 500th anniversary – 6 July 1915 – of his being burnt at the stake. On the east side of the square is the Hussites' main church, the **Church of Our Lady Before Týn** ③ *(Chram Matky Boží před Týnem)*, with its iconic twin towers, known as Adam and Eve (one is shorter and thinner than the other).

Round the back of the church is the **Týn Court**, the origins of which go back to the 11th century, when it offered protection to foreign merchants. It is now a beautiful setting for cafés and

Left: Old Town Square.

tyrdom in 1415. Hus's quarters are next door and accommodate an exhibition on his life and work.

On the west side of Bethlehem Square is an archway leading to the **Ethnographic Museum** ⑤ *(Náprstkovo muzeum)*, housing Asian, African and American collections in a former brewery.
SEE ALSO CHURCHES, P.47; MUSEUMS AND GALLERIES, P.87

Josefov

The northern section of Staré Město forms the Jewish Quarter. Here, the **Jewish Museum** maintains the **Old Jewish Cemetery** ⑥ and five historic synagogues. It is also the location of a small exhibition on Franz Kafka, author of *The Trial*, who lived and worked in the district.

Kafka's place of worship, the **Old-New Synagogue** ⑦ *(Staronová synagoga)* does not form part of the Jewish Museum. Dating back to the 1270s, it is the oldest Jewish house of worship still in use in Europe. Inside you can still see the seat of Rabbi Löw (1525–1609), the supposed creator of the mythical Golem.
SEE ALSO JEWISH PRAGUE, P.70, 71; LITERATURE AND THEATRE, P.74

some unusual shops selling puppets, antique books and toiletries.
SEE ALSO CHURCHES, P.47; MONUMENTS, P.79, 80

Clementinum

At the western end of Staré Město is the Clementinum, founded by Jesuits in 1556. They had been called to Prague by the Habsburgs to cancel out the revolutionary ideas promulgated by the Protestant Charles University. As their wealth grew so did their new religious precinct.

Today the Clementinum is part of the university, housing its **National Library**. You can visit the **Baroque Library Hall** with its painted ceiling, the **Astronomical Tower** above it and the **Chapel of Mirrors** – a venue for concerts.
SEE ALSO ARCHITECTURE, P.26

Southern Staré Město

In the south of the Old Town are the earliest buildings of

the Charles University or 'Karolinum' centred around Gothic **Rotlev House** at no. 9 Železná. Founded by Charles IV in 1348, the university became associated with the Protestant reformers – Jan Hus was rector from 1402.

Just nearby is the neoclassical **Estates Theatre** ④ *(Stavovské divadlo)*, where Mozart conducted the premiere of *Don Giovanni* in 1787.
SEE ALSO LITERATURE AND THEATRE, P.76

Bethlehem Square

In the southwest of Staré Město is Bethlehem Square *(Betlémské náměstí)*. On the north side of the square is the **Bethlehem Chapel** *(Betlémská kaple)*, where Jan Hus delivered his fiery Reformationist sermons (in Czech rather than Latin) from 1402 until shortly before his mar-

Right: the Astronomical Clock.

Nové Město

Prague's 'New Town' was laid out in the early 14th century by Charles IV. It has a very different feel to the narrow streets of Staré Město or Malá Strana. Its streets are lined with grand 19th-century buildings, not least the National Theatre, and including some fine examples of Art Nouveau architecture. Among these imposing façades are some little gems to search out. There are some important churches, including a restored Gothic cloister, a Functionalist building for an artists' association on an island in the river, a lovely botanical garden and a museum to one of the Czechs' greatest composers, Antonín Dvořák.

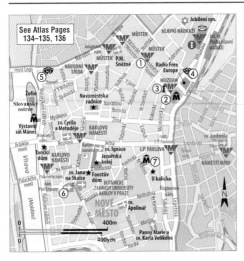

though the city authorities are slowly waking up to the need for renewal. A competition has led to the appointment of architect Jakub Cigler to restore the square's fortunes. SEE ALSO ARCHITECTURE, P.29

The National Museum

At the square's southeastern end is the the **National Museum** ② (*Národní Muzeum*). In front it, with a commanding position, is the equestrian **Statue of St Wenceslas** ③, and close by, two small mounds in the cobbled pavement mark the place where the students Jan Palach and Jan Zajic set fire to themselves in 1969 in protest against Soviet oppression.

Wenceslas Square

Wenceslas Square ①
(*Václavské náměstí*) is actually more of a broad boulevard than an open square. Sloping down at the heart of Nové Město, its wide pedestrian zones follow the course of the fortifications that surrounded the city in the Middle Ages, before Charles IV erected the New Town in a semicircle around the old. At the end of the 19th century and beginning of the 20th century many fine Art Nouveau and Functionalist buildings and arcades were built around the square.

Although the square was originally used as a horse market, it eventually became the setting for much grander events. All of Prague's historic uprisings – from the Reformationist Hussite Rebellion in the early 15th century to the nationalist riots in 1848 to the remarkably peaceful Velvet Revolution in 1989 – have focused on the square.

Since those heady days, however, the square has lost some of its lustre. Burger bars, casinos, strip clubs, souvenir stalls and parked cars now set the tone,

On the corner of Resslova is Frank Gehry and Vlado Miluničis Nationale Nederlanden Administrative Building, aka the **Tančící dům**, also nicknamed the 'Fred and Ginger' building on account of its supposed likeness to a dancing couple. It was built in 1992–6, and its post-modern quirkiness now seems a little dated. However, it does have a pleasant small bar and café on the ground floor, and its rooftop restaurant has wonderful views over the city. *See also Architecture, p.27.*

Left: Looking down Wenceslas Square.

the **New Town Hall** *(Novoměstská radnice)* and to the south is the **Faust House** *(Faustův dům)*. According to legend, this was once the residence of the German magician and alchemist Dr Faustus, famed for selling his soul to the devil in exchange for power and knowledge.

On Resslova, towards the river, is the Orthodox **Church of SS Cyril and Methodius** *(Kostel sv. Cyrila a Metoděje)*. Below, in the crypt, is the **National Memorial to the Heroes of the Heydrich Terror** *(Národního památníku hrdinů heydrichiády)*, a display telling the story of the seven men who held out here after the assassination of Reichsprotektor Richard Heydrich.

SEE ALSO CHURCHES, P.49

Just to the east of the National Museum (along Wilsonova) is the old Stock Exchange building. This was transformed into a glass structure to house the Federal Assembly in 1966–72. It now houses Radio Free Europe, and as such requires concrete barriers and armed guards. Just beyond it is the **State Opera House** ④ *(Státní Opera Praha)*, and beyond that, **Hlavní nádraží**, the city's Art Nouveau main railway station.

SEE ALSO MONUMENTS, P.81;
MUSEUMS AND GALLERIES, P.91;
MUSIC, P.101

Our Lady of the Snows and National Theatre

On Jungmannovo náměstí at the top of Národní is a **Cubist lamppost** (designed by Emil Králíček in 1913) outside the gate of the Franciscan rectory. Behind this is the **Church of Our Lady of the Snows** *(P.M. Sněžné)*.

At the far end of Národní by the river is the neo-Renaissance **National Theatre** ⑤ *(Národní divadlo)*, which opened in the 1880s. Along the riverbank is Masarykovo nábřeží, lined with elegant *fin de siècle* buildings.

Facing Masarykovo nábřeží is the wooded **Slavic Island** *(Slovanský ostrov)*, home to the **Žofín** concert hall. At the far end of the island is the **Mánes House** *(Výstavní síň Mánes)*, an excellent example of Functionalist architecture.

SEE ALSO ARCHITECTURE, P.26;
CHURCHES, P.49; LITERATURE AND
THEATRE, P.76

Karlovo Náměstí and a National Memorial

Just up from the riverbank is the large open space of **Karlovo náměstí**. This was built during the construction of the New Town and was once the site of the cattle market. On the north side is

The Emmaus Monastery and Dvořák Museum

On Vyšehradská, south of the square, is the **Emmaus Monastery** ⑥ *(Klášter na Slovanech)* with its Gothic cloisters, partially destroyed during World War II. At the bottom of Vyšehradská, past the Baroque **Church of St John on the Rock** *(sv. Jana na Skalce)*, is the entrance to the **University Botanical Gardens**.

Up the hill to the left of the gardens, on Ke Karlovu, is the Villa Amerika, now housing the **Dvořák Museum** ⑦ *(Muzeum Antonína Dvořáka)*. To the south are many departments of the city's university and, at the far end of Ke Karlovu, **Church of the Virgin Mary and Charlemagne** *(Panny Marie a sv. Karla Velikého)*.

SEE ALSO CHURCHES, P.49;
MUSEUMS AND GALLERIES, P.90;
PARKS AND GARDENS, P.110

Vyšehrad

Vyšehrad is a rocky hill that rises from the place where the Vltava reaches the old city limits. According to legend it was here, in her father's castle, that Princess Libuše had her vision of the golden city of Prague: 'I see a great city, whose fame will reach to the stars… there in the woods you shall build your castle and your settlement, which shall be named Praha.' Archaeologists doubt the veracity of this tale as Prague Castle was built in the 9th century and Vyšehrad was erected in the 10th century. But in the second half of the 19th century, at the peak of the Czech national revival, the story was irresistible to artists and composers.

History

Vyšehrad (literally 'high castle') has played a key role in Prague's history since the Přemyslid kings established it as their seat of power. Its tumultuous career as a battle fortress began in 1004, when it repelled the invading forces of Poland's Boleslav the Brave. Over the years the royal residence alternated between Vyšehrad and Hradčany, and the hill was repeatedly ransacked by foreign armies. Today, by contrast, the monuments of Vyšehrad are set in attractive parkland.

The Congress Centre and Tábor Gate

Between Vyšehrad metro station and the **Vyšehrad National Cultural Monument** (Vyšehrad Národní Kulturní Památka) is the imposing communist-built **Congress Centre** ① (Kongresové-Centrum), formerly known as the Palace of Culture. Walk in front of the centre and descend the short flight of stairs onto Na Bučance and follow the signposts that lead towards Vyšehrad. Soon, past the 14th-century ramparts, you turn turn right into the **Tábor Gate** (Táborská brána). Just beyond the gate is an **Information Centre** housed in the remains of the **Špička Gate** (Špička brána).

Churches and the Cemetery

Ahead is the 17th-century **Leopold Gate** (Leopoldova bána) and, to the right, the **St Martin's Rotunda** ②

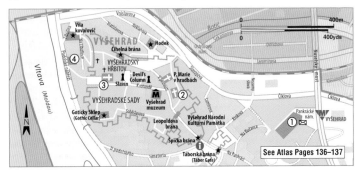

See Atlas Pages 136–137

Left: the Cubist Villa Kovařovič. **Far left:** view of the Vltava River.

fully known as the 'Baths of Libuše' – jutting out of the rock were once the outpost towers from which sentinels kept watch over the Vltava.

The Descent

To descend to the embankment of the river there are two choices. You can return to the road in front of the cemetery and, near the medallion to the geologist Jan Krejčí, take the precipitous steps on the western side of the hill to the Vltava. The other way is to retrace your steps to St Martin's Rotunda, turn left and descend past the Church of St Mary in the Ramparts to the **Cihelná Gate** *(Cihelná brána)*. This will bring you out near the Hodek *(see below)*.

Cubist Houses

If you descend from near the cemetery you will pass above a splendid example of Cubist housing by the architect Josef Chochol: the **Cubist Triple House** ④, built in 1913–14. At the bottom of the steps, on the corner of Rašínovo nábřeží and Libušina, and nearby on Neklanova, are two more wonderful buildings by Chochol, the **Villa Kovařovič** (1912–13) and the **Hodek** (apartment house; 1913–14).

(Rotunda sv. Martina). This is a tiny Romanesque church dating from the 11th century, sensitively restored in the 1870s, and one of the oldest in the country.

To the left, on K rotundě with its low stone walls, is a lawn on your right where three short stone columns lean against each other at odd angles. These are known as the **Devil's Column** *(see box, below right)*.

Further on is the well-tended **Vyšehrad Park** *(Vyšehradské sady)* and the **Church of SS Peter and Paul** ③ *(Kostel sv. Petra a Pavla).* This twin-spired building is largely notable for its Art Nouveau paintings of the saints. There has been a church here since the 11th century, but the present neo-Gothic construction dates to 1885.

Nearby lies the **Vyšehrad Cemetery** *(Vyšehradský hřbitov)*, laid out in 1870. This is the resting place of numerous national figures, including the composers Smetana and Dvořák, the writers Jan Neruda and Karel Čapek, and the artist Alfons Mucha. A large monument, the **Slavín** is a communal grave for some of the greatest Czech artists.
SEE ALSO CHURCHES, P.50; PARKS AND GARDENS, P.110

River Views

Through the stone gate opposite the cemetery is a wide lawn with four monumental statues by the sculptor Jan Myslbek. The statues depict characters from Czech legends, including Libuše herself. Further along is the former summer palace of Emperor Charles IV. Also here is the **Gothic Cellar** *(Goticky Sklep)*, home to a well-displayed permanent exhibition on the history of the site.

There is wonderful view over the river and the city from the battlements. The remnants of buildings – fanci-

> There is a religious legend associated with the three columns of the **Devil's Column**. It is said that a priest bet the devil that he could say Mass before the devil could deliver a column from St Peter's Basilica in Rome. The devil took a column from a closer church, but St Peter intervened, waylaying the devil and breaking the pillar in three.

15

Smíchov and the Southwest

In the 18th century, Smíchov was outside the city, favoured by the aristocracy for their summer retreats amongst the fields and vineyards. Manor houses, villas and lodges, such as that now housing the Mozart Museum, were then commonplace. By the 19th century, however, Prague was expanding fast, and Smíchov came to house the overspill. It was incorporated in 1838 and became a focal point of Czech industrialisation. Breweries were built on the banks of the Vltava, a railway hub was constructed, and the area became a working-class enclave. Today, by contrast, in the post-industrial age, the district has a relaxed feel, with shops, cafes and pedestrianised areas.

Anděl

At the heart of Smíchov is **Anděl metro station**. It was built as a communist showpiece and used to be known as *Moskevská* (Moscow) – a gesture of friendship towards the Soviet Union, and a point hammered home with a number of large murals showing triumphant workers striding into the future. Opposite the platforms, you can still see today eight bronze reliefs, one showing two cosmonauts, another with a young girl waving flags marked *Moskva* and *Praha*.

Ascending the escalators, you emerge, ironically, into the **Nový Smíchov Shopping Centre** ①, a showpiece of the new capitalist Prague and

the largest and flashiest mall in the city. The name 'Anděl' means 'angel', and so the centre's architect, Jean Nouvel, has had a 21st-century angel depicted on the glass façade, along with quotations (in red writing) from Czech literature, including from the works of Franz Kafka.

SEE ALSO SHOPPING, P.123

Bertramka Villa

Walk due west of Anděl and you come to Mozartova, a leafy lane that takes you uphill to the gateway of the **Mozart Museum** ② *(Muzeum W.A. Mozarta Bertramka).*

Once a vineyard manor house, the property later became the country villa of František Dušek and his young

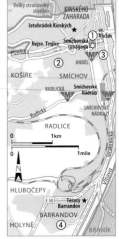

wife (he was old enough to be her father), the singer Josefina Dušková. It was here that Mozart stayed on his visits to Prague in 1787 and 1791, and here that he composed the aria *Bella mia fiamma, addio* from *Don Giovanni* for Josefina. He also, allegedly, scrawled out the overture to the opera the night before its premiere at the Estates Theatre in the city centre. Sadly, the original villa was largely destroyed by fire on New Year's Eve 1872–3. It was

Left: mural at Anděl station.

Left and below: Nový Smíchov Shopping Centre.

Staropramen Brewery

The Staropramen Brewery ③ is currently the second-largest in the Czech Republic. Its construction began in 1869 and the first beer was brewed in 1871. Facing onto Nádražní at no. 84 is the brewery's own pub and restaurant, where you can sample 10 different varieties of its product. It is also possible to see the inside of the brewery, with guided tours on offer daily.

SEE ALSO FOOD AND DRINK, P.60; RESTAURANTS, P.118

Barrandov Studios

Films have been made at the Barrandov Studios ④ since 1932, when they were founded by the Havel brothers (one of them the father of the future Czech president), and in their first decade made up to 80 films a year. During World War II, the studios were confiscated by the Nazis, who exploited the facilities to make pictures that promoted Nazi values. After the war, the studios were nationalised and remained under state ownership until the 1990s. Since then, Barrandov has been the filming location for numerous Hollywood blockbusters.

SEE ALSO CINEMA, P.52

Just behind Anděl metro station, on the corner of Plzeňská and Stroupežnického, is an interesting synagogue, the **Smíchovská Synagoga**. Founded in 1863, it was given a Modernist makeover in 1931 by Leopolda Ehrmanna and then completely renovated and reopened in 2004 (with an excellent second-hand bookshop attached).

finally reconstructed in 1941.

Today, the building functions as a museum, and an exhibition of musical instruments, manuscripts and memorabilia pays tribute to Mozart and the musical culture in which he operated.

SEE ALSO MUSEUMS AND GALLERIES, P.92

Štefánikova and Nádražní

Returning to Anděl metro station again, if you head north on Štefánikova, you will eventually arrive at Malá Strana. Shortly on the right, however, is the barn-like **Church of Sv. Václav**, built from 1881 to 1885 to designs by Antonín Barvitius. Next to the church is the **Portheimka**, a small 18th-century mansion built by Kilián Ignaz Dientzenhofer (one of the architects of St Nicholas's Church in nearby Malá Strana) as his town residence. Behind it is the small park of náměstí 14 října.

Heading south of Anděl, though, the road becomes Nádražní. Before long on the left is the enormous Staropramen Brewery, and if you continue south, you come to the railway station, **Smíchovské nádraží**. Built in 1854, it was revamped in 1947 to designs by Jan Zázvorka and Jan Žák with an imposing Socialist-Realist façade. Some way further south still are the Barrandov Film Studios.

Holešovice and Troja

The districts of northern Prague (sometimes referred to by their post-code as Prague 6) comprise Holešovice and Troja. Often ignored by tourists, they contain some of the city's most important and interesting sights. There is the exceptional modern art collection housed in the Veletržní palác, the museum of one the Czech Republic's most important sculptors, as well as a couple of interesting exhibitions currently undergoing an extensive renovation. Holešovice also contains some of the most extensive areas of parkland in the city, and to the north in Troja are the city's Botanical Gardens.

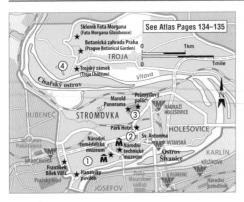

Holešovice

The district of Holešovice is a 19th-century suburb (incorporated into the city in 1884), now a little run-down but with elegant and decorated late 19th-century apartment buildings. The district lies to the northeast of Hradčany and is separated from the castle district by the wide expanse of **Letná Park** ① (*Letenské sady*). This is where the statue to Stalin was erected in 1953–5, dominating the whole city; when Krushchev came to power, however, it proved an embarrassment and was subsequently demolished.

A number of museums can be found around Letná. Near the southern end of the park is the **Villa František Bílek**, the house of the eponymous sculptor and now a museum dedicated to his works. On the northern edge of the park are the **National Technical Museum** (*Národní technické muzeum*), at present closed for a major reconstruction, and the **National Museum of Agriculture** (*Národní zemědělské muzeum*).
SEE ALSO MUSEUMS AND GALLERIES, P.96; PARKS AND GARDENS, P.110

ST ANTHONY AND THE TRADE FAIR PALACE

Not far from Vltavská metro station is Strossmayerovo náměstí. Here is the **Church of St Anthony**, modelled on the Týn Church in Staré Město *(see p.10)*.

Along Dukelských hrdinů is one of the most important modern buildings in the city, the **Trade Fair Palace** ② (*Veletržní palác*), one of the earliest large-scale Functionalist buildings in Europe. It now holds the **National**

Left: Letná Park.

Left: Lapidarium.

(pronounced 'Troya'). It can be reached either by tram from Výstaviště or bus 112 from Nádraží Holešovice metro. A more pleasant way, however, is to walk through the Stromovka park, crossing under the railway line and then taking the footbridge to **Emperor's Island** (Císařský ostrov). From here another footbridge brings you out onto the far bank of the river.

Facing onto the river are the walls of the gardens of the **Trojský zámek** (Troja Château), a large Baroque mansion open to the public.

Opposite the main entrance to the château is the way into **Prague Zoo** ④, chiefly of interest to families. On the hillside above the château is a large vineyard. This is part of the **Prague Botanical Gardens** (Botanická zahrada Praha), an extensive area of greenery and very pleasant to wander around. Perhaps the most impressive attraction here is the **Fata Morgana greenhouse** with its different climatic zones.

SEE ALSO CASTLES, PALACES AND HOUSES, P.38; CHILDREN, P.40; PARKS AND GARDENS, P.110

Designed by Oldřich Tyl and Josef Fuchs, the **Trade Fair Palace** was built in 1924–8 and was admired by Le Corbusier. He saw in it how his own large-scale projects might be realised, while qualifying his enthusiasm by saying, 'It's an interesting building but it's not yet architecture.'

Gallery of Modern Art.
SEE ALSO CHURCHES, P.50; MUSEUMS AND GALLERIES, P.93

Výstaviště and the Lapidarium

Further on, past the communist-era Park Hotel, is Prague's main exhibition ground at **Výstaviště**. Still used for trade shows and exhibitions, as well as the occasional rock or pop concert, the exhibition ground is dominated by the large and ornate **Průmyslový palác**, one of the finest Art Nouveau buildings in Prague. However, much of the left wing was destroyed in a fire in October 2008, and the authorities are still debating whether to rebuild the wrecked structure.

Beside the Průmyslový palác is the building of the National Museum's **Lapidarium** ③ (collection of sculpture), closed at present for a revamp. Close by is the 19th-century **Marold Panorama** of the battle of Lipany.
SEE ALSO MUSEUMS AND GALLERIES, P.92, 93

STROMOVKA

Behind Výstaviště is a large area of parkland. This is **Stromovka**, originally a royal hunting ground and one of the largest parks in the city.
SEE ALSO, PARKS AND GARDENS P.111

Troja

The area to the north of the Vltava is known as **Troja**

Right: Trade Fair Palace.

Bubeneč, Střešovice and Břevnov

The western reaches of the city stretch from just behind the castle to the airport on the outskirts at Ruyzně. Like the other outer stretches of Prague they are relatively unexplored by tourists, but they more than repay the – minor – effort of exploring them. One the city's most interesting sights is the Müller Villa, a beautiful house designed by Adolf Loos, and there is also a fun transport museum, large parks and an extraordinary Renaissance palace.

Bubeneč

Bubeneč, to the north of Hradčanská metro, is a district consisting of large villas and *fin de siècle* bourgeois apartments. As such – and much like Střešovice *(see right)* – it is

> The **Battle of the White Mountain** took place on 8 November 1620, and the Protestant forces of Frederick V were defeated by the imperial Catholic armies led by Johann Tserclaes Graf von Tilly. From this point until 1918 Bohemia became part of the Habsburg Empire and entered a period of Catholic domination, disastrous for the Czech Protestant population but giving the ensuing Catholic Habsburg patronage a blessing for Prague's legacy of Baroque architecture.

home to diplomats, embassies and high-ranking civil servants. The district covers the western end of Stromovka, and merges further west into the estates that surround Vítězné náměstí (by Dejvická metro).

North of the huge square, along Jugoslávských partyzánu, is the imposing **Hotel International** ①, one of the great Stalinist monuments of the city.
SEE ALSO ARCHITECTURE, P.29

THE BABA ESTATE

On the hillside above the hotel is one of the great examples of Czech Modernist architecure, the Baba Estate of the Czechoslovak Werkbund. Built between 1928 and 1940, these are some of the finest examples of Modernist housing to be found anywhere.

SEE ALSO CASTLES, PALACES AND HOUSES, P.39

Střešovice

Behind Hradčany is Střešovice, similar in feel to the upmarket parts of Bubeneč. Here, at Patočkova 4, is the **City Transport Museum** ② *(Muzeum městské hromadné dopravy)*, a collection of trams and trolleybuses. Not far away, at Nad hradním vodojemem 14, is the **Müller Villa** *(Müllerova vila)*, the only example of the work of Brno-born architect Adolf Loos in Prague.
SEE ALSO CASTLES, PALACES AND HOUSES, P.39; MUSEUMS AND GALLERIES, P.97

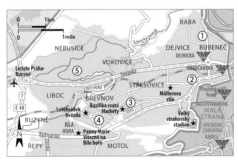

Right: Letohrádek hvězda.

Left and far left: Břevnov Monastery.

field, reached by a footpath from either Nad višňovkou or Řepská. Although there is little to see, the view is extensive and the site can appear suitably desolate in bad weather. Looking north from the monument you can see the wall of the **Obora hvězda** ④ (park) surrounding the star-shaped **Letohrádek hvězda**.
SEE ALSO CHURCHES, P.51

OBORA HVĚZDA

Taking the tram back into town and alighting at the Vypich stop brings you to the edge of the park. In the centre of the park is one of the most interesting Renaissance buildings in the city, the **Letohrádek hvězda**, a six-pointed palace.
SEE ALSO CASTLES, PALACES AND HOUSES, P.39; PARKS AND GARDENS, P.111

Břevnov

To the west, in the district of Břevnov, is the **Břevnov Monastery** ③ *(Břevnovský klášter)*. This is the oldest monastery in Prague, founded in 993.
SEE ALSO CHURCHES, P.50

BÍLÁ HORA

The site of the Battle of the White Mountain (Bílá Hora,

see box, left) is at the terminus of tramlines 8 and 22. Just beside the tram terminus is the attractive **Church of Our Lady of Victory** *(Panny Marie Vítežné na Bílé hoře)*.

The site itself (take the road on the right just after the church and follow it uphill) is marked by a small stone in the middle of a

Divorká Šárka

To the north of Ruzyne, location of the city's airport, and Břevnov is the **Prírodní Rezervace Divorká Šárka** ⑤, a wild expanse of parkland.
SEE ALSO PARKS AND GARDENS, P.111

Vinohrady and Žižkov

The two eastern suburbs of Vinohrady and Žižkov form one of the most diverse parts of Prague, from elegant *fin de siècle* apartments to local pubs and ivy-covered cemeteries. These districts of Prague are fascinating, and their 19th- and 20th-century buildings make a change from the Gothic- and Baroque-dominated areas in the centre of the city. They vary in feel from an ex-pat, arty chic to gritty working-class sleaze. Impressive monuments are not lacking either, the east being home to two of the most imposing in the city, the National Monument, with its huge statue of Jan Žižka, and the Žižkov Television Tower.

Vinohrady

The district of **Vinohrady** gets its name from the vineyards that once thrived here. Today it is a pleasant, lively area, full of young, upwardly mobile Czechs, who live in the *fin de siècle* apartment blocks that make up much of the area.

ST LUDMILA AND NÁMĚSTÍ MÍRU

At the heart of Vinohrady is the large square of **náměstí Míru**, lined with late 19th-century apartments, and also with the newly restored Art Nouveau **Vinohrady Theatre** *(divadlo na vinohradech)*. At the centre of the square is the large neo-Gothic church of **Church of St Ludmila** *(Svatá Ludmila)*.
SEE ALSO CHURCHES, P.51

To the east and southeast of Vinohrady and Žižkov there is little of specific interest to visitors. The areas from Prague 4 (Podolí and Hodkovičky) across to Prague 11 (Chodov) are dominated by *paneláky*, prefabricated concrete tower blocks that were put up in the 1960s and 70s as a solution to a chronic housing shortage, and now form a rather characterless and uniform urban sprawl.

Right: Olšany Cemetery.

PARKS

The district of Vinohrady is bordered by two parks, both within walking distance of náměstí Míru metro. The **Reiger Gardens** ① *(Riegrovy sady)* are to the north, while to the south are the **Havlíček Gardens** *(Havlíčkovy sady)*. Also here is the **Gröbovka**, a 19th-century villa by the architect Antonín Barvitius.
SEE ALSO PARKS AND GARDENS, P.111

CHURCH OF THE SACRED HEART

On náměstí Jiřího z Poděbrad (by the metro station of the

same name) is the most unusual Modernist building in Prague, **Church of the Sacred Heart** ② *(Nejsvě-tějšího Srdce Páně)*, designed

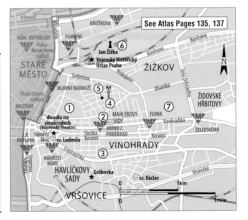

See Atlas Pages 135, 137

Left: the Akropolis arts centre.

immense granite-faced cube containing the Tomb of the Unknown Soldier. In front of it stands one of the biggest equestrian statues in the world, the **monument to the Hussite leader Jan Žižka**.

On the way up the hill you pass the **Museum of Military History** *(Vojenský Historický Ústav Praha)*. The walk up through the park is pleasant, and the views from the top of the hill are wonderful.

SEE ALSO MONUMENTS, P.79; MUSEUMS AND GALLERIES, P.97

CEMETERIES

The other sites of interest in Žižkov lie further out, but are easily accessible by either tram or metro. The first of these is **Olšany Cemetery** ⑦ *(Hřbitov Olšany)*. This huge necropolis has been the preferred burial spot of many famous Czechs (particularly if they have not managed to get a spot in Vyšehrad, *see p.15*).

Just beyond this cemetery is the **Židovské Hřbitovy, New Jewish Cemetery**. It is just as impressive as the Olšany Cemetery, perhaps even more so, with its attractive, tree-lined avenues of graves overgrown with ivy.

SEE ALSO JEWISH PRAGUE, P.71; PARKS AND GARDENS, P.111

by the architect Josip Plečnik (who was responsible for the restoration of St Vitus's).

For those in search of more Modernist churches, two other treats lie in the east of the city: Josef Gočár and Alois Wachsman's **Church of St Wenceslas** *(Sv. Václav)*, and Pavel Janák's **Hussite Cathedral** ③ *(Husův sbor)*.

SEE ALSO CHURCHES, P.51

Žižkov

A sometimes seedy district of run-down apartment blocks, **Žižkov** (Prague 3) lies to the north of Vinohrady and stretches out to the eastern edge of the city. Its working-class credentials are well established, and it was at one time a hotbed of sedition. It is also famous for its huge number of basic local pubs (more than any other district of Prague), not all of which are welcoming or salubrious. One of the more friendly places is **U vystřelenýho oka** (The Shot-

Out Eye), named after the Hussite leader Jan Žižka, who gives his name to the district.

THE TELEVISION TOWER

On **Mahler Park** *(Mahlerovy sady)*, dominating the entire district – and much of the city – is the **Prague Television Tower** ④ *(Televizní vysílač Praha)*. Easily visible from the tower (looking north) is a colourful apartment block on the nearby corner of Kubelíkova and Víta nejedléno. This is the **palác Akropolis** ⑤, an arts centre set in the prewar Akropolis theatre.

SEE ALSO LITERATURE AND THEATRE, P.77; MONUMENTS, P.81; NIGHTLIFE, P.104

THE NATIONAL MONUMENT

Also to the north and dominating Žižkov Hill above Husitská is the **National Monument** ⑥ *(Národní památník)*. The National Monument is an

Right: Television Tower.

A–Z

In the following section Prague's attractions and services are organised by theme, under alphabetical headings. Items that link to another theme are cross-referenced. All sights that are plotted on the atlas section at the end of the book are given a page number and grid reference.

Architecture

rague exhibits an extraordinary variety of architectural styles. Having suffered only light bombing in World War II, its stock of medieval, Gothic, Rococo, Baroque, neoclassical, Art Nouveau, Art Deco, Cubist, Modernist and communist-era is remarkably well preserved. This chapter provides a selection of fine examples of different styles, though readers should also consult the sections on *Castles, Palaces and Houses* (especially for the Müller Villa and the Baba Estate), *Churches* (not least for St Nicholas's Church and the Emmaus Monastery) and *Museums and Galleries* for the Villa František Bílek.

Clementinum

Křížovnické náměstí; precinct open daily 6am–11pm; free; tram: 17, 18, 53, metro: Staroměstská; map p.134 A3

The Clementinum monastic complex is situated at the Staré Město end of the Charles Bridge. The college was founded in 1556 by the Jesuits, who had been summoned to the country by the Habsburgs to spearhead the Counter-Reformation and cancel out the revolutionary ideas promulgated by the Protestant Charles University (of which Jan Hus had once been rector). As the Jesuits' wealth accrued, they bought up churches, gardens and 30 houses to extend their precinct.

In 1773, however, not long after the buildings were finally completed, Josef II forced the Jesuits into exile in enthusiastic compliance with the Pope's decree to suppress the order (it had become a political liability). Today, the Clementinum is part of Charles University and accommodates four libraries and a concert venue.

Enter by the gate just to the left of the Baroque façade of **St Salvator** (completed in 1601, though modified by Carlo Lurago around 1650). Cross the first courtyard and walk through the arch. Immediately on your

left is the **National Library** with its collection of 6 million volumes. On your right is the **Church of St Clement**, which is often open to the visitors. Its exuberant Baroque interior was designed by Kilián Dientzenhofer between 1711 and 1715. It now ministers to a Greek Orthodox congregation. Just behind it is the oval-shaped **Italian Chapel**, which can be seen from the street outside, but is closed to the public. Built around 1590 for the Italian craftsmen working in the complex, it is

Prague even has a **Cubist lamppost**, designed by Emil Králíček in 1913. It can be found on at Řijna 28 (near Jungmannovo náměstí) outside the gate of the Franciscan rectory connected to the Church of Our Lady of the Snows.

Left: Cubist traditions are well represented in Prague.

the tower and a cannon let off. The **Chapel of Mirrors** is a frequent venue for concerts, during which you can gaze at Jan Hiebl's frescoed ceiling, with its strips that illustrate verses of the Hail Mary prayer, and Václav Vavřinec Reiner's murals of scenes from the life of the Virgin Mary. To exit the complex walk through the gate to the far right hand corner of the courtyard into Marianské náměstí.

Dancing Building

Rašínovo nábřeží 80; not open to the public; tram: 17, 21, metro: Karlovo Náměstí; map p.136 A2

Constructed in 1996 by architects Vlado Milunič and Frank Gehry, this office building – colloquially known as

still technically owned by the Italian government.

At the far end of this second courtyard is the Astronomical Tower on your left. Entrance to the **Baroque Hall** is just beneath it, and entrance to both can be gained through one of the guided tours on offer (tel: 222 220 879; daily, tours on the hour from 10am, last tour at 7pm; charge). Tickets can be purchased at the Mirrored Chapel (which is also included in the tour) in the next courtyard, through the arch on the left.

The **Baroque Library Hall** was completed in 1722 and ever since has housed a collection of theological books (those with whitened backs and red marks date back to the Jesuit period). The allegorical ceiling frescoes by Jan Hiebl depict antique learning as the basis for Christian teachings.

Above the library is the **Astronomical Tower**, also built in the 1720s and used for observation of the skies right up until the 1930s. Halfway up you can see the Prague meridian; when sunlight crossed the line at noon, a flag used to be hung from

Left: The Clementium.
Right: The Dancing Building.

'Fred and Ginger' – has become an emblem of the changing city. Occupying a site left by an American bomb that fell in World War II, the glass tower is hugged into the starchier 'Fred Astaire' half of the building. The reason for the pinched-in glass section was said to be so that the neighbouring building retained its view of Prague Castle. The uncharitable have likened it to 'a crushed Coke can'.

Municipal House (Obecní dům)

Náměstí Republiky 5; tel: 222 002 101; www.obecnidum.cz; daily 10am–11pm; free; tram: 5, 8, 14, 51, 54, metro: Náměstí Republiky; map p.134 C3

This extravagant Art Nouveau building was built between 1905 and 1911 and houses a fine concert hall and several restaurants. The large arched façade features a huge mosaic by Karel Špillar called *Homage to Prague*. Inside, every surface is covered with murals, tiles or more mosaic, and some of the paintings are by Alfons Mucha, the master of Art Nouveau.

SEE ALSO RESTAURANTS, P.116

In the 1970s and 80s large estates of high-rise apartment blocks were built in Prague's suburbs. They were constructed of prefabricated concrete panels, earning them the generic name *paneláky* in Czech. Unlike in many Western European countries, these estates proved surprisingly successful, attracting residents from a variety of social segments and generating a strong social cohesion. The most intact estates can still be seen in the southeast of the city in Jižní Město (metro: Hajé).

Powder Gate (Prašna brána)

Na Príkope; tel: 724 063 723; Apr–Oct 10am–6pm; admission charge; tram: 5, 8, 14, 51, 54, metro: Náměstí Republiky; map p.134 C3

Although situated next door to the Municipal House, this exercise in Gothic could not be more different. Built in 1475 on the site of one of the original 13 gates into the Old Town, it was modelled on the Old Town Bridge Tower and at first was known as the New Tower. It marked the beginning of the Royal Way (*see Staré Město, p.10*). It assumed its current name in the early 18th century when it was used to store gunpowder. The building was remodelled between 1875 and 1886, when it was given its steeple. Inside, you

Right: Wenceslas Square.

Left: Powder Gate and Municipal House.

Beginning at the top (southern) end, there is the neo-Renaissance **National Museum** built to designs by Josef Schulz, from 1885 to 1890. Continuing down the right-hand side of the square, you come to the **Hotel Evropa** at nos 25–7. This grand Art Nouveau establishment is the result of Alois Dryák's makeover of the building in 1905 (with the assistance of architectural sculptor Ladislav Šaloun). The hotel's magnificent interior was used in the film *Mission Impossible*.

Opposite, on the other side of the square at no. 36, is the **Melantrich Building**, built in 1914. It was on the balcony here on 24 November 1989 that Alexander Dubček and Václav Havel appeared together before a crowd of 300,000 people in a pivotal event of the Velvet Revolution. The building is now occupied by Marks and Spencer. Just nearby, at no. 34, is the **Wiehl House**, built in 1896 to designs by Antonín Wiehl. Its extravagant façade is decorated with neo-Renaissance murals by Czech artist Mikuláš Aleš and others.

Tucked away behind, in the block between Štěpánská and Vodičkova, is the labyrinthine **Palác Lucerna** shopping arcade. This Art Nouveau complex harbours the gorgeous **Lucerna cinema** (operating since 1909) and associated bar (now somewhat louche, though it retains its stylish décor). Hanging from the ceiling of the arcade's atrium is David Černy's sculpture of King Wenceslas on his upside-down horse, a satire on the monumental version in the square outside.

Continuing down the square, there is Ludvík Kysela's **Alfa Palace** at no. 28 and Pavel Janák's **Hotel Juliš** at no. 22 – both 1920s Modernist affairs. Then there is the Art Nouveau **Peterka House** at no. 12, built to Jan Kotěra's designs in 1899–1900, and close by at no. 8, Blecha and Králíček's **Adam Pharmacy** (built 1911–13). At no. 6 is the city's earliest concrete-framed building, built in 1929 to the Functionalist designs of Ludvík Kysela. His patron was Tomáš Baťa, the progressive industrialist who founded the shoe empire. Another of Kysela's creations – the **Lindt Building** – can be found at no. 4.

SEE ALSO CINEMA, P.52; MONUMENTS, P.81; MUSEUMS AND GALLERIES, P.91

can see an exhibition about the city's towers and climb the 186 steps to reach the viewing platform and see over the surrounding rooftops.

Wenceslas Square

Václavské náměstí; tram: 3, 9, 11, 14, 24, metro: Můstek, Muzeum; map p.134 B4/C4

Wenceslas Square forms a survey of the architectural styles of the last 150 years.

The most striking example of Stalinist architecture in the city is the former **Hotel International** (now the Crowne Plaza; Koulova 15; tel: 222 254 007; metro: Dejvická then tram: 8). It was built in 1951–6 and designed by František Jeřábek. Its monolithic structure, crowned with a spire and red star, is decorated with Socialist-Realist friezes. The impressive, if somewhat heavy, interior is beautifully finished.

Cafés and Bars

Prague is blessed with fine cafés in the grand Viennese style and jolly pubs in the Northern European tradition. The city's café culture exhibits a mode of architecture and decoration all of its own, reaching its apogee in extravagant establishments such as the Café Slavia or Café Imperial. Prague's pubs and beerhalls benefit from a distinguished brewing history, and the temperature of the city's ancient cellars – ideal for the preservation of Pilsner – ensure a perfect, cool, clear product every time. Of course, Prague also has some fun cocktail bars, and a selection of the best are listed in the Nightlife section *(see p. 102–5)* of this book.

Malá Strana

Bohemia Bagel
Lázeňská 19; tel: 257 218 192; www.bohemiabagel.cz; daily 7.30–11pm; tram: 12, 20, 22, 23, metro: Malostranská; map p.133 C2

Dependable American-style café, serving fresh bagels and sandwiches, cooked breakfasts (until 2pm), pancakes, muffins, salads, quiches and burgers. Free refills of coffee and soft drinks. Wine and beer also on offer. Internet access available.

Cukrkávalimonáda
Lázeňská 7; tel: 257 530 628; www.cukrkavalimonada.cz; daily 8.30am–8pm; tram: 12, 20, 22, 23, metro: Malostranská; map p.133 C2

'Sugar-coffee-lemonade' is a beautifully styled café offering variations around scrambled eggs for breakfast, then pastas, frittatas, pancakes and sandwiches throughout the day, and then Mediterranean-style meals in the evening – salmon tagliatelle, chicken and prosciutto, trout and thyme. Try also the home-made pastries and cakes and speciality hot chocolate.

Savoy Café
Vítězná 5; tel: 257 311 562; www.ambi.cz; Mon–Fri 8am–10.30pm, Sat–Sun 9am–10.30pm; tram: 12, 20, 22, 23; map p.133 D3

Smart and stylish café-restaurant for breakfast, lunch, dinner, or just coffee and cake. The menu includes fried eggs with black truffle, steak tartare, and cottage cheese dumplings stuffed with fruit.

Left: Café Slavia, Prague's most famous and historical place for a coffee.

Café Slavia
Národní třída/Smetanovo nábřeži; tel: 224 218 493; www.cafeslavia.cz; daily 8am–11pm; tram: 6, 9, 17, 18, 21, 22, 23, 53; metro: Národní Třída; map p.134 A4

This famous café, with its views over the river and National Theatre, was once the haunt of artists and writers, including Václav Havel. The spacious and elegant Art Deco interior encourages you to linger, and morning coffee turns into lunch with a range of salads, pancakes and Czech dishes.

Ebel Coffee House
Týn 2; tel: 224 895 788; www.ebelcoffee.cz; daily 9am–10pm; tram: 5, 8, 14, 51, 54; map p.134 B3

This café, situated in a courtyard behind the Týn Church, offers some of the best coffee in Prague, with a large variety of roasts. All of these can be bought, along with a wide variety of teas, at their nearby shop Vzpomínky na Afriku (on Rybná/Jakubská). The café also serves a selection of light meals.

U Hrocha
Thunovská 20; tel: 222 516 978; daily 11am–11pm; tram: 12, 20, 22, 23, metro: Malostranská; map p.133 C2

'The Hippo' is one of the few places in the district still aimed at local residents. Simple wooden furniture, a smoky atmosphere, excellent beer and basic high-carb food to soak up the alcohol.

U Kocoura
Nerudova 2; tel: 257 530 107; daily 11am–11pm; tram: 12, 20, 22, 23, metro: Malostranská; map p.133 C2

'The Tomcat' pub used to be owned by the Friends of Beer, which was once a political party, but now merely a civic association. Despite its location near Malostranské náměstí, its prices are very reasonable.

Hradčany

U Černého Vola
Loretánské náměstí; tel: 220 513 481; daily 10am–10pm; tram: 22, 23; map p.132 B2

Left: streetside cafés in Staré Město.

The Black Ox is an old-fashioned beer hall serving fine, dark Velkopopovický Kozel beer to locals.

Staré Město

Café Imperial
Na poříčí 15; tel: 246 011 440; www.cafeimperial.cz; daily 7am–11pm; tram: 5, 8, 14, 51, 54, metro: Náměsti Republiky; map p.135 C2

One of the grand old cafés of Prague, the Café Imperial is worth a visit just for the newly restored Art Nouveau interior with its wonderful tiling. Breakfast, lunch, afternoon tea and evening meals are served by friendly staff.

Café Montmartre
Retězová 7; tel: 222 221 244; Mon–Fri 9am–11pm, Sat–Sun noon–11pm; tram: 17, 18, 53, metro: Staroměstska; map p.134 A3

Historic café, once frequented by writers such as Jaroslav Hašek and Egon Erwin Kisch. Though no longer a hotbed of political and cultural debate, it remains a pleasant place to sit, read and drink.

Prague pubs come in various shapes and sizes. The most basic is the *hostinec* or *pivnice* – beer house – which is a simple watering hole that also serves simple food. Next up the ladder is the *hospoda*, the pub or beer hall. Most pubs are tied to a particular brewery, serving its product on draught in half-litre glasses. Many *hospody* serve perfectly good meals, and those at the top end of the scale may be little different from *restaurace* (restaurants).

Káva Káva Káva

Národní třída 37; tel: 224 228 862; www.kava-coffee.cz; Mon–Fri 7am–10pm, Sat–Sun 9am–10pm; tram: 6, 9, 17, 18, 21, 22, 23, 53, metro: Národní Třída; map p.134 A4

A pleasant, quiet café in a courtyard opposite Tesco. The friendly staff serve excellent coffee in vast mugs as well as a selection of bagels, quiches and cakes. There is also internet access downstairs.

Krásný Ztráty

Náprstkova 10; tel: 775 755 143; www.krasnyztraty.cz; Mon–Fri 9am–1am, Sat–Sun noon–1am; tram: 17, 18, 53, metro: Staroměstska; map p.134 A3

Stylish and informal café-cum-wine-bar-cum-gallery also hosting literary evenings and concerts. Breakfasts include bacon and cheese, and yoghurt and fruit. The rest of the day, choose from quesadillas, lasagne, sausages, salads, vegetarian dishes, honey cake and ice cream.

U Zlatého tygra (The Golden Tiger)

Husova 17; tel: 222 221 111; www.uzlatehotygra.cz; daily 3–11pm; tram: 17, 18, 53; metro: Staroměstska; map p.134 A3

Perhaps the most famous hostelry in Prague, this was where Václac Havel took Bill Clinton in 1994 to show him a real Czech pub. Unfortunately, since then it has put up its prices and gone for the tourist dollar. Even so, its cellars still provide ideal conditions for the storage of the Pilsner dispensed upstairs.

> The coffee house was one of the great institutions of the inter-war First Republic. Some have faded into history – for example, the Arco, meeting place of 'Arconauts' Kafka, Werfel and Max Brod. Others are still in business, such as the Café Slavia (see p.31), filled in its heyday with poets, painters, and actors from the National Theatre opposite.

Café Slavia (see p.31)

Nové Město

Café and Galerie Louvre

Národní třída 20; tel: 224 930 949; www.cafelouvre.cz; daily 8am–11.30pm; tram: 6, 9, 17, 18, 21, 22, 23, 53, metro: Národní Třída; map p.134 B4

An elegant Art Nouveau café, much loved in the past by Prague's intellectuals, this is a great place to sit and browse through the papers. Below the café proper is a café-gallery displaying contemporary art, while upstairs you can get good-value breakfasts and light meals throughout the day.

Globe Bookstore and Coffeehouse

Pštrossova 6; tel: 224 934 203; www.globebookstore.cz; daily 9.30am–midnight; tram: 17, 21; map p.136 A1

Well known as a centre of expat intellectual life. As well as the friendly café, with good coffee and light meals (pasta, salads and burgers), the bookshop has occasional live music, lectures and book-

Left: The Globe Coffeehouse is an ex-pat hub.

is a welcome haven from the brash commercialism of Wenceslas Square. As well as excellent coffee, the café serves light snacks, wines and beers (including Polička – very good). Friendly service.

Vyšehrad
U Neklana
Neklanova 30; tel: 224 916 051; daily 11am–midnight; tram: 7, 18, 24, 53, 55
Neighbourhood pub on the ground floor of a fine Cubist building dating from 1915. Serves simple Czech dishes and Budvar beer.

Smíchov and the Southwest
Hostinec U Váhy
Nádražní 88; tel: 257 326 539; Mon–Fri 10am–11pm, Sat–Sun noon–10pm; 6, 9, 12, 20, 58, metro: Anděl
This unaffected working man's pub serves Gambrinus beer, so you can perform a 'compare and contrast' with the product at the Staropramen brewery next door. Serves good honest grub as well.

Holešovice
U Houbaře
Dukelských hrdinů 30; tel: 222 982 430; Mon–Sun 11am–midnight; tram: 5, 12, 14, 15, 17, 53, 54, metro: Vltavská
Straightforward pub, serving Pilsner Urquell and simple Czech meals to a regular lunchtime crowd: fried cheese, pork steaks, dumplings.

Břevnov
Letena Park Beer Garden
Letenské sady 341; tel: 233 378 208; www.letenskyzamecek.cz; daily 11am–11pm; tram: 1, 25, 26
Situated at the other end of the park from the Pavilon restaurant, this white stucco mansion houses several eateries, although this beer garden is the main draw.

Vinohrady and Žižkov
Kavárna Medúza
Belgicka 17; tel: 222 515 107; www.meduza.cz; Mon–Fri 10am–1am, Sat–Sun noon–1am; metro: Náměstí Míru
Old-fashioned and a little eccentric, this coffee house is decked out with creaky old furniture and paintings by local artists. It serves a wide variety of alcoholic and non-alcoholic drinks as well as simple meals.

readings and signings. It is also one of the most pleasant, and cheapest, places to check your email.
SEE ALSO LITERATURE AND THEATRE, P.75
Kavárna Evropa
Václavské náměstí 25; tel: 224 228 117; www.evropahotel.cz; 9.30am–11pm; metro: Můstek; map p.134 C4
The magnificent Art Nouveau interior of this café gives a taste of old-world style. The food, however, is decidedly mediocre and overpriced, so stay only as long as you need to take in the atmosphere.
Kavárna Řehoř Samsa
Vodičkova 30 (pasáž U Nováků); tel: 224 225 413; 9.30am–7pm; tram: 3, 9, 14, 24, 52, 53, metro: Můstek; map p.134 B4
This bookshop-cum-café takes its name from the protagonist of Kafka's *Metamorphosis*. Tucked away in one of the passages off the Lucerna shopping arcade, it

Right: Café Louvre.

Castles, Palaces and Houses

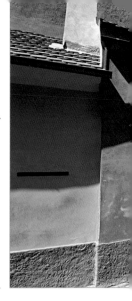

The silhouette of Hradčany (the castle district) is perhaps the best-known view of the city. With the advantage of its exposed position, the castle dominates the skyline of the left bank of the Vltava. It is particularly impressive when floodlit at night, with the cathedral in the background. Malá Strana has a number of fine Baroque palaces, many now home to foreign embassies. Prague's notable architecture is not, however, all Gothic and Baroque, as there are some splendid examples of early Modernism.

Malá Strana

Wallenstein Palace (Valdštejnský palác)

Valdštejnské náměstí 4; tel: 257 071 111; www.senat.cz; Sat–Sun 10am–5pm; free; tram: 12, 18, 20, 22, 23, 57, metro: Malostranská; map p.133 C2

The Wallenstein Palace was the first Baroque palace in Prague, built 1624–30 for General Albrecht von Wallenstein. The grandiose residence matches Wallenstein's grand political ambitions, and it was intended to rival Prague Castle which looms above. Wallenstein acquired the site for the building by buying up and dispossessing the inhabitants of more than 20 houses. Even the city gate had to go, in order to give the architects (all Italians) enough space to provide their patron with a luxurious palace. Today it is the home of the Czech Senate, but some access is allowed to the public.

The rooms that are open include the Mannerist and early Baroque main hall, with superb ceiling paintings by Baccio di Bianca. Off the main hall is the Knights' Hall, with its unusual 19th-century leather wall covering, which leads on to the ornate circular Audience Chamber and mythological passage decorated with scenes from Ovid and Virgil.
SEE ALSO PARKS AND GARDENS, P.108

Hradčany

Černín Palace (Černínský palác)

Loretánské náměstí; no access to the public; metro: Malostranská; map p.132 B2

Opposite the Loreta is the massive façade of the Černín Palace. Some 29 half-pillars run along the whole length of the palace façade, which is more than 150m (492ft) long.

In 1666, Johann Humprecht, Count Czernin von Chudenitz, bought the land, and work started on the palace, under the direction of Francesco Caratti. In 1673, Emperor Leopold I came to Prague to see the building about which there was so much talk in Vienna. It seemed as if the count, who had not received the imperial favour he expected, was building a palace out of pique. The emperor was displeased when the count

Left: Wallenstein Palace.

Left: Prague Castle's Golden Lane.

Prague's royal residence matches its imposing appearance. Its history is not only tied up with that of the city, but also with the history of the first independent Czech state and its destiny. The castle is the seat of the president of the republic and still a centre of political power.

The building of the castle dates from the same period as the first historically documented prince of the Přemyslid dynasty, Prince Boleslav. He built what was at first a wooden fort on the site of a pagan place of worship. It then became the seat of the dynasty and secured the crossroads of important European trade routes which met at the ford of the Vltava. At the same time, Boleslav

claimed that it was nothing but a barn and he was going to replace the wooden doors with bronze ones. 'For a barn, those wooden doors are quite good enough,' the emperor is reported to have said.

The Černín were an old Bohemian family, and their members had long been in the service of the Bohemian crown. The house in Prague was to become a monument to the power of the family, and construction work continued for several generations until financial collapse put a stop to the project. During the Napoleonic Wars it was used as a military hospital, and in 1851 the state bought parts of it and turned it into a barracks. In 1929, the authorities of the young Czechoslovak Republic had the palace renovated and made it the home of the Foreign Ministry, which it still is today. It was here that Jan Masaryk fell – or was pushed – to his death in 1948.

Lobkowicz Palace (Lobkovický palác)

Jiřská 3; tel: 233 312 925; www.lobkowiczevents.cz; daily 10.30am–6pm; admission charge; metro: Malostranská; map p.132 C1

Also within the castle complex is the Lobkowicz Palace. The palace has been returned to its original owners, the Lobkowiz family, one of the ancient princely dynasties of Bohemia, and owners of the largest private art collection in the country. Once displayed at their Renaissance residence in the village of Nelahozeves, many of these treasures are now on view here. They include fabulous paintings such as *Haymaking*, the only one of Pieter Brueghel the Elder's depictions of the seasons of the year which is in private ownership. Among reminders of the family's lavish patronage of music and musicians are manuscripts by Mozart and Beethoven, and there is also an extensive collection of arms and armour.

Prague Castle (Pražský Hrad)

Hradčany; tel: 224 373 368; www.hrad.cz; daily Apr–Oct 9am–6pm, Nov–Mar 9am–4pm; admission charge; metro: Malostranská; map p.132 C2–C1

The historical importance of

A fair number of Malá Strana's palaces are now home to foreign embassies. The magnificent Baroque Lobkovický palác on Vlašská is home to the German Embassy. On Tržiště is the Schönbornský palác, which now houses the heavily guarded US Embassy (all passing cars are stopped and searched). It has a splendid garden, which can be seen from the castle. On Nerudova is the Morzinský palác, the Romanian Embassy. Its unusual façade – the heraldic Moors which support the balcony, the allegorical figures of Day and Night and the sculptures representing the four corners of the world – are the work of Ferdinand Maximilian Brokoff. Higher up is the Thun-Hohenštejnský palác, the Italian Embassy, which is decorated with two eagles with outspread wings, and is the work of Matthias Bernard Braun. The statues of Roman deities represent Jupiter and Juno.

built the first church on the hill to replace the pre-Christian burial ground, as a sign of progressive Christianisation. In AD 973, when the bishopric of Prague was founded, the castle also became the bishop's seat.

After AD 1000 a Romanesque castle gradually evolved on the site, with a princely (later a royal) palace, a bishop's palace, several churches, two monasteries and a series of fortifications. Every period has added its contribution to the castle's development, but its appearance today is due mainly to Empress Maria Theresa.

TICKETS

Tickets for entry to the castle buildings are sold in the Third Courtyard in the **Information Centre of Prague Castle**. Two different tickets are available (a long tour and a short tour, both valid for two days), covering: the Old Royal Palace, the Story of Prague Castle, St George's Basilica, St George's Convent (the National Gallery's collection of 19th-century Bohemian art), Golden Lane and Daliborka Tower, the Castle Picture Gallery and the Powder Tower.

THE FIRST AND SECOND COURTYARDS

The main entrance to the castle is the **První nádvoří**

(First Courtyard), which opens onto Hradčany náměstí. You enter this so-called Ceremonial Courtyard through a gate under a wrought-iron decoration. Two guards of honour are posted in front of the statues, copies of the *Battling Titans* by Ignaz Platzer.

This is the most recent of the courtyards and was built on the site of the western castle moat during the alterations of Maria Theresa's reign (1740–80). The **Matthias Gate** (*Matyášova brána)* is considerably older; indeed, it is the oldest Baroque building in Hradčany Castle. It originally stood apart, like a triumphal arch, between the bridges that led over the moats. During the rebuilding it was elegantly integrated into the new section as a relief. Since then, the Matthias Gate has been the entrance to the Second Courtyard. To the right of the gate a staircase leads to the reception rooms of the presidential apartments, which are closed to the public.

The **Druhé nádvoří** (Second Courtyard) has a somewhat plain appearance. In the centre is a Baroque fountain by Hieronymus Kohl (1686). In the southeastern corner is the **Chapel of the Holy Cross** *(Kaple sv. Kříž)*, built 1756–63 by Anselmo Lurago.

It now serves as a shop and a box office selling tickets for concerts.

The symmetrical, closed impression given by the Second Courtyard is thanks to Maria Theresa's innovations. Behind it, however, lies a conglomeration of buildings which has grown up gradually over the centuries. Each has its own complicated history. In the right-hand passage to the Third Courtyard you can see some excavated remains of the Romanesque castle fortifications. The remains of an even older building, **St Mary's Church**, dating from the 9th century, were discovered in the Prague Castle Picture Gallery.

OLD ROYAL PALACE

The **Old Royal Palace** (*Staré královský palác)* was also built by many generations of rulers. New storeys of the palace were layered one above the other on top of the original walls, which now lie deep under the level of the courtyard. It is possible to visit a large part of the palace, which until the 16th century was the residence of the Czech rulers.

Access is via an anteroom, the entrance to which is on the eastern side of the Third Courtyard. From the anteroom you enter the

Left: details from Prague Castle.

Vladislav Hall *(Vladislavský sál)*, named after King Vladislav II. This imposing late Gothic throne room was built by the architect Benedikt Ried between 1493 and 1502. Numerous coronations and tournaments took place under the 13m (43ft) high vaults. Immediately to the right of the entrance of this hall another wing of the building is joined.

Continue on the same level and you reach the Bohemian Chancellery. Go through a Renaissance doorway and you enter the office of the former Imperial Governor. Ascending a spiral staircase, you come to the Imperial Court Chancellery. This is situated above the Bohemian Chancellery; in Rudolf II's reign, the whole of the Holy Roman Empire was ruled from here.

Under the three Renaissance windows on the far wall of the Vladislav Hall a staircase leads to a gallery overlooking the **All Saints Chapel**, which contains three remarkable works of art: *Triptych of the Angels* by Hans von Aachen; *All Saints*, the painting on the high altar, by Václav Vavřinec Reiner; and, in the choir, a cycle of paintings by Dittmann. The last

portrays 12 scenes from the life of St Procopius, who is buried in the chapel.

The next room leading off from the Vladislav Hall is the **Council Chamber**, in which the Bohemian Estates and the highest law court assembled. The royal throne and the furnishings date from the 19th century. To the left of the throne is the tribunal of the chief court recorder, built in the Renaissance style. The wall is decorated with portraits of the Habsburg rulers.

The last room open to the public in this wing is the **New Land Records Office**, above the Council Chamber, with the heraldic emblems of the Land Rolls officials decorating the ceiling and walls.

The **Riders' Staircase**, built to allow rulers and guests to enter and take part in events on horseback such as jousting, leads out of the most recent part of the palace. The early Gothic levels on the lower storeys are accessible as part of the 'Story of Prague Castle' exhibition, as is the lowest level, the Romanesque palace which contains the remains of fortifications dating from the end of the 9th century.

THE STORY OF PRAGUE CASTLE
This beautifully displayed exhibition can be reached by

the ramp to the left of the entrance to the Old Royal Palace. It makes a highly recommended introduction to the castle site (see www.pribeh-hradu.cz) and has two parts: the first leads you from room to room describing the development of the castle in chronological order; the second tells the 'Story of…' various subjects, such as residences, learning, burials, the Church and patronage.

The story of the castle site is told from prehistory to the 20th century. Among the exhibits that illustrate the history of the castle are a helmet and chainmail coat said to have belonged to St Václav; the tympanum of the **Basilica of St George** *(Bazilika sv. Jiří)*; the grave dresses of Rudolf II and Eleonora of Toledo; and some amazing examples of 16th- and 17th-century costume.

Staré Město

Clam-Gallas Palace (Clam-Gallasův palác)
Archivni 6; tel: 236 001 111; www.ahmp.cz; admission by

The **changing of the guards** *(left)* at Prague Castle always draws a crowd, especially at midday when it is accompanied by music. Far from being steeped in military tradition, this faintly ludicrous Ruritanian ceremony was invented after 1989. The uniforms, dripping with braid and tassels, were designed by Theodor Pištěk (the English pronunciation of his surname is suspiciously appropriate), who was responsible for the costumes in *Amadeus*. The Hollywood feel is enhanced by the trumpets, trombones and tuba playing from surrounding windows; the score, composed by Michal Prokop, sounds like a bad soundtrack to a war movie.

prior appointment; metro: Staroměstská; map p.134 A3
The Clam-Gallas Palace is a magnificent Baroque building (1713–30) constructed by the Viennese court architect Johann Bernhard Fischer von Erlach. The door ornamentation of statues of Hercules is by Matthias Bernhard Braun. Once containing a theatre, where Beethoven reputedly performed, the building now houses the city archives.

Goltz Kinsky Palace (Goltz-Kinských palác)
Staroměstské náměstí 12; tel: 224 810 758; www.ngprague.cz; Tue–Sun 10am–6pm; admission charge; tram: 17, 18, 53, metro: Staroměstská; map p.134 B3
This late Baroque palace was designed by Kilián Ignaz Dientzenhofer in February 1948. It was from here that communist leader Klement Gottwald made the speech that brought in the totalitarian regime. The building houses the National Gallery's collection of landscape painting from the 17th–20th century.
SEE ALSO MUSEUMS AND GALLERIES, P.87

House of the Black Madonna (Dům u černé Matky Boží)
Ovocný trh 19; tel: 224 211 746; www.ngprague.cz; Tue–Sun 10am–6pm; admission charge; metro: Náměstí Republiky; map p.134 B3
The Cubist House of the Black Madonna was designed by Joseph Gočár (1911–12), originally as a department store. The second to fourth floors contain the National Gallery's Museum of Czech Cubism.
SEE ALSO MUSEUMS AND GALLERIES, P.87

Troja

Trojský zámek
U trojského zámku 1; tel: 283 851 614; www.citygallery prague.cz; Sat–Sun 10am–5pm; admission charge; bus: 112

On the narrow street of Melantrichova in Staré Město is the Dům u dvou zlatých medvídů (**House of the Two Golden Bears**). Its door is a beautiful example of Renaissance architecture.

Built 1679–85 by Jean-Baptiste Mathey for Václav Vojtěch of Sternberg, this large Baroque mansion has an ornate interior covered in frescoes on classical themes. The château and gardens suffered greatly in the 2002 floods, but much of the damage has now been repaired. Approaching through the gardens from the river gives you a view of the southern façade, with its staircase decorated by monumental sculpture representing the battle between the gods and Titans.

When you enter the building you will be given a pair of overshoes, designed to protect the floors. The château is home to a collection of 19th-century Czech painting, the best of which are probably the landscapes on display in the first few rooms. Many of the same artists are represented as in the National Gallery's collection in the Klášter sv. Jiří. Of particular interest are Ludvík Kohl's highly Romantic *Gothic Hall with a Meeting of a Secret Brotherhood* (1812);

Left: Letohrádek hvězda in Obora hvězda park.

two lovely landscapes of mountain waterfalls by Charlotta Peipenhagenová (1880s); a *Forest Scene* (1853) by Josef Mánes; and the virtuoso *Path in a Deciduous Forest* by Bedřich Havránek (1878).

The rooms upstairs have particularly fine decoration, the most impressive being the Grand Hall, completely covered in frescoes by Abraham Godyn (1663–1724).

Bubeneč, Střešovice and Břevnov

The Baba Estate of the Czechoslovak Werkbund

Baba; bus 131 from Zelená, alight at Matějská

On the hillside above Dejvice is one of the great examples of Czech Modernist architecture, the Baba Estate. Built between 1928 and 1940, these are some of the finest examples of Modernist housing to be found anywhere. Although none of the buildings are open to the public, it is still interesting to wander around the quiet streets of the estate.

It displays a unity at odds with the way it developed. After the basic infrastructure and ground plan of the area (by Pavel Janák) had been set out, each house was commissioned separately and the individual plans were discussed between the architect and client. With the exception of the Dutch architect Mart Stam, the others were all drawn from the Czechoslovak Werkbund, which included some of the finest architects of its day: Janák, Josef Gočár and Ladislav Žák. Notable buildings include the Čeněk Villa (Na Babě 11, by Žák, 1932),

the Janák House (Nad Pat'ankou 16, 1931–2) and the Palička House (Na Babě 9, by Stam and Jiří Palička, 1929–32).

Letohrádek hvězda

Obora hvězda; tel: 220 612 229; www.oborahvezda.webpark.cz; Tue–Sun May–Sept 10am–5pm, Oct–Apr 10am–4pm; admission charge; tram: 8, 22

At the centre of the Obora hvězda park is the Renaissance Letohrádek hvězda. The six-pointed structure was designed by Hans Tyrol and Bonifac Wohlmut in 1555 for Archduke Ferdinand of Tyrol. On the ground floor, as well as some beautiful stucco work on the ceilings, there are exhibits describing the palace and its restoration by Pavel Janák. In the basement is a huge model of the Battle of Bílá Hora, while on the first floor is a fascinating exhibition on the mystical significance of the star; unfortunately, like all the exhibits, it is only labelled in Czech.

Müller Villa (Müllerova vila)

Nad hradním vodojemem 14; tel: 224 312 012; www.mullerova vila.cz; guided tours only that must be booked in advance, Tue, Thur, Sat–Sun Apr–Oct 9am, 11am, 1pm, 3pm, 5pm, Nov–Mar 10am, noon, 2pm, 4pm; admission charge; tram: 1, 2, 18

The Müller Villa is the only example of the work of architect Adolf Loos in Prague. The villa was designed and built in 1928–30 for the wealthy couple František and Milada Müller. As befits an iconic Modernist building, the exterior is plain and severe, but the beautifully designed interiors are luxurious.

The tour, limited to around seven people at a time, is very informative and lasts around one hour. It takes you

One of the most important architects of early Modernism, Adolf Loos was born in Brno in 1870, then part of the Austro-Hungarian Empire. He trained in Vienna and, after a short period in North America, soon established a reputation as an iconoclast, particularly following the publication of his most influential work, *Ornament and Crime*, in 1908. This outlined his ideas on decoration (he repudiated it), which were put into effect in one of his most important buildings, the Michaeler House (1909–11) in Vienna. The blank, featureless façade was revolutionary and even raised the ire of the emperor, who had to look out on it from the Hofburg. He carried these ideas over into the construction of domestic architecture, notably in the Steiner House (Vienna, 1910) and the Müller Villa *(see left)* in Prague.

through all the public and private areas of the villa, and even down into the basement to see the heating system.

Now the villa has been restored to its former glory it is possible to see just how well laid out the building is and how colour is used as an element in the organisation of the overall design. Particularly appealing elements are the open-plan living room with its large windows and a dining space above, the 'boudoir', a cosy space which acted as a private retreat, and the elegant lady's dressing room. The heating system and utility rooms show just how well integrated Loos's design was. Next door to the boiler room is the laundry, with long racks that pull out to dry the clothes using the heat from the boiler for both the hot water and drying.

Children

The Czech Republic retains a family-orientated ethos, and Prague itself offers an old-fashioned childhood experience with funfairs and playgrounds, a zoo and an aquarium, transport and toy museums, puppet theatres and even a hall of mirrors. Among the few concessions to late 20th-century childhood experience are Laser Quest and a host of fast-food restaurants. Apart from the attractions listed below, the very fabric of the city also provides sustenance for young imaginations: a grand castle, church steeples, cobbled lanes and fairytale burghers' houses.

Children's Attractions

Laser Game
Národní 25; tel: 224 221 188; www.lasergame.cz; daily 10am–midnight; admission charge; tram: 6, 9, 18, 21, 22, 23, 51, 54, 57, metro Národní Třida; map p.134 A4
Located within the Metro-Palác shopping complex, this Laser Quest labyrinth enables children to zap their parents all day, every day.

Mirror Maze
Petřín Hill; tel: 257 315 212; Jan–Mar, Nov, Dec Sat, Sun 10am–4.45pm, Apr, Sept daily 10am–7pm, May–Aug daily 10am–10pm, Oct 10am–6pm; admission charge; tram: 12, 20, 22, 23, 57 then funicular; map p.132 B3
On the outside, this cast-iron mock-Gothic castle has its own drawbridge and turrets. Inside, there is a hall of distorting mirrors as well as a wax diorama of the battle between the Praguers and the Swedes in 1648 on the Charles Bridge.

Prague Zoo (Zoologická zahrada v Praze)
U Trojského zámku 3; tel: 296 112 111; www.zoopraha.cz; daily Jan–Feb and Nov–Dec 9am–4pm, Mar until 5pm, Apr–May and Sept–Oct until 6pm, Jun–Aug until 7pm; admission charge; tram: 14, 17, metro: Nádraží Holešovice, then bus 112
Gorillas, giraffes, hippos and their friends can all be seen in this zoo in the Troja area of Prague.

St Matthew's Fair (Matějská pout)
Výstaviště; tel: 220 103 204; www.matejskapout.cz; late Feb–mid-Apr Tue–Fri 2–10pm, Sat–Sun 10am–10pm; tram: 5, 14, 25, metro: Vltavská
For a good month and a half, a funfair – with carousels, dodgems and candy floss stands – is added to the Ferris wheel and rollercoaster of Lunapark.

> Museums that might appeal to children include the **Aircraft Museum** *(see p.89)*, the **City Transport Museum** *(see p.97)*, the **National Technical Museum** *(see p.96)* and the **Toy Museum** *(see p.86)*.

Left: kids will especially enjoy the exhibits at the City Transport Museum, *see p.97*.

Left: changing shape at the Mirror Maze.

Sea World (Mořský svět)
Výstaviště; tel: 220 103 275; www.morsky-svet.cz; daily 10am–7pm; admission charge; tram: 5, 12, 14, 15, 17, metro Nádraží Holešovice
Aquarium housing over 300 species, including sharks, tropical fish, crustacea and turtles.

Playgrounds
Children's Island
Dětský ostrov, access from Nábřeží; tram: 6, 9, 12, 20, 22, 23; map p.133 D4
This island just off Kampa Park in Malá Strana has slides and swings, sandpits and children's sports facilities.
Jungleland
Výmolova 298; tel: 251 555 149; daily 9am–7pm; admission charge; metro: Radlická
Large indoor playground for children under 13 years. Slides, bridges, tunnels, Wendy houses, balls and hoops provide the amusement.
Kinský Gardens
Újezd 1; tram: 6, 9, 12, 20, metro: Anděl; map p.132 C4

In the grounds of the Kinský Summer Palace, this playground can be found by following the paths to the right on entering the park.
SEE ALSO MUSEUMS AND GALLERIES, P.87
Petřín Hill
Petřín Hill; tram: 12, 20, 22, 23, 57 then funicular; map p.132 B3
By the Seminary Garden (with its blossoming fruit trees) on the east slope of the hill, is a playground, with slides and climbing frames on a large sandy area.
SEE ALSO PARKS AND GARDENS, P.108

Puppet Theatre
National Marionette Theatre
Žatecká 1; tel: 224 819 322; www.mozart.cz; box office open daily 10am–8pm; tram: 17, 18, 53, metro: Staroměstská; map p.133 E2
Puppet performances of Mozart operas.
Theatre Minor
Vodičkova 6; tel: 222 231 351; www.minor.cz; box office open Mon–Fri 10am–1.30pm and 2.30–8pm, Sat–Sun 11am–8pm; tram: 3, 9, 14, 24, metro: Karlovo Náměsti; map p.136 B1
Recently built theatre putting on wonderful productions (without words) of myths and fairy tales.
Theatre of Spejbl and Hurvínek
Dejvická 38; tel: 224 316 784; www.spejbl-hurvinek.cz; box office open Tue, Thur–Fri 10am–2pm, 3–6pm, Wed until 7pm, Sat–Sun 1–5pm; tram: 1, 2, 5, 8, 18, 20, 25, 26, metro: Dejvická, Hradcanská
Home to puppets Spejbl and Hurvínek since 1930, this theatre puts on magical stories for adults and children.

Left: waiting to take the stage.

Churches

Although not a conspicuously pious people, the Czechs have been witness to, or instigators of, many of the great religious upheavals of the past 1,000 years. These range from the Hussite rebellion to the establishment of the Catholic hegemony during the Counter-Reformation. These religious movements have left their mark on the city with great monuments, and Prague's Baroque churches are some of the finest in Central Europe. Perhaps the greatest religious monument of all, however, is the Gothic Cathedral Church of St Vitus, perched on top of Hradčany and dominating the city.

Malá Strana

Church of Our Lady Beneath the Chain (Kostel Panny Marie pod řetězem)
Lázeňská; tel: 257 530 876; Mon–Sat 9.30am–5pm; free; tram: 12, 20, 22; map p.133 C2–D2

On the junction between Lazeňská and Maltézské náměstí is the Church of St Mary Beneath the Chain, the oldest church in Malá Strana. The 12th-century remains of its Romanesque predecessor can still be seen in the right-hand wall of the forecourt. The church behind, with a beautiful Baroque interior, was built in the 17th century by Carlo Lurago.

Church of St Mary Victorious (Kostel Panny Marie Vítězná)
Karmelitská 9; tel: 257 533 646; www.pragjesu.info; daily 8.30am–7pm; free; tram: 12, 20, 22; map p.133 C2

The Church of St Mary Victorious was begun in 1611 and was Prague's first, though by no means its best, Baroque church. After the Battle of the White Mountain it was confiscated from its Protestant congregation and soon became a stronghold of the Counter-Reformation brought to the city by the Habsburgs. The furnishings, which are all of a unified style, date from the 17th century; the saints' pictures by the altar are the work of Petr Brandl.

Church of St Nicholas (Chrám sv. Mikuláše)
Malostranské náměstí 29; tel: 251 512 516; daily Mar–Oct 9am–5pm, Nov–Feb 9am–4pm; admission charge; tram: 12, 20, 22; map p.133 C2

The conspicuous dome of St Nicholas and its slender tower dominates Malá Strana.

Left: Basilica of St George.

It is in the Church of St Mary Victorious that the famous **Bambino di Praga** is kept, a 16th–17th-century wax figure of Spanish origin of the infant Jesus, dressed in one or another of its 72 costly robes, some of which are on display in the upstairs museum. This rather unpreposessing little figure is revered by Catholics, and believed to work miracles, thus ensuring a constant stream of pilgrims, many of them from the countries of Latin America.

This is Prague's greatest Baroque building; it has recently undergone a restoration and its spectacular interior is bright and gleaming. It is also possible to ascend the tower – a favourite lookout of the secret police during the communist years – with its great view over the surrounding rooftops.

In the early 18th century the famous Bavarian architect Christoph Dientzenhofer built the nave and side chapels on the site of a Gothic church. The choir and the dome were added later by his son Kilián

Left: many of Prague's churches are rich in detail.

of the church. A beautifully ornate example of Central European Baroque, the church originally had two altarpieces by Rubens *(The Martyrdom of St Thomas and St Augustine)*, now replaced by copies (the originals are in the National Gallery). The ceiling frescoes are by the Bohemian artist Václav Vavřinec Reiner.

Hradčany

Basilica of St George (Bazilika sv. Jiří)
Náměstí sv. Jiří; tel: 224 373 368; www.hrad.cz; daily Apr–Oct 9am–6pm, Nov–Mar 9am–4pm; admission charge; metro: Malostranská; map p.133 C1

St George's Basilica is the oldest church still extant on the site of the castle and, together with the adjoining monastery, it formed the hub of the complex in the early Middle Ages. It was founded in about AD 920 and rebuilt after a fire in the 12th century. Despite rebuilding programmes during the Renaissance and Baroque periods, the church has largely retained its Romanesque appearance and, following renovations at the beginning of the 20th century, it has been restored to its former glory.

The interior is closed off by a raised choir. Remnants of the original Romanesque ceiling paintings can still be seen. To the right of the choir you can look through a grille into the **Ludmilla Chapel**, housing the tomb of the saint, the grandmother of Prince Wenceslas.

The tombs of two Bohemian nobles are in front of the choir. The Baroque statue in front of the crypt – a

Ignaz. The building was completed in the mid-18th century by the addition of the tower, which was the work of Carlo Lurago.

Particularly outstanding among the special features of the interior is the monumental ceiling fresco by Johann Lukas Kracker in the nave. It is one of the largest in Europe and portrays scenes from the life of St Nicholas. Another valuable fresco, *Celebration of the Holy Trinity* by Franz Xaver Karl Palko, decorates the dome. The dome is 75m (246ft) high. A particularly fine view of the ceiling frescoes – and indeed the whole interior – can be had from the gallery above the nave (the entrance to the steps lies to the left of the main altar).

The impressive sculptures of the Eastern Church Fathers that stand in front of the four supporting pillars of the dome (clockwise from the right St Cyril Alexandrijsky, Jan Zlatoústý, Řehoř Naziánský and Basil Veliký, 1755–69) are the work of František Ignác Platzer. He was also responsible for the

gilded statue of St Nicholas (1765) which is by the high altar. The wooden altar was designed by Andrey Pozza and dates to the first quarter of the 18th century. Also worthy of note is the stunningly ornate pulpit, made of artificial marble and covered with gilt (from the workshop of R.J. Prachner, 1762–6).

St Thomas (Sv. Tomáše)
Josefská 8; 221 714 444; Mon–Sat 11am–1pm, Sun 9am–noon, 4.30–5.30pm; free; tram: 12, 20, 22; map p.133 C2

The entrance to the church and former monastery of St Thomas is on a small road off to the left on Letenská. The famous monastic brewery (founded in 1358) is no longer in existence and its equally famous beer cellar is under reconstruction. The church is the most impressive part of the former Augustinian monastery, and was first built in the 13th century. Its present Baroque form (late 1720s) is the work of Kilián Ignaz Dientzenhofer.

However well conceived it is on the outside, it is the interior that is the finest part

Right: The Loreta.

corpse with snakes in its intestines – is an allegory of the transitory nature of life. The Baroque **Chapel of St John Nepomuk** is incorporated into the outer façade of the basilica. Its door is decorated with a 17th-century statue of the saint by Ferdinand Maximilian Brokoff.

The Loreta

Loretánská náměstí; tel: 220 516 740; www.loreta.cz; Tue–Sun 9am–12.15pm, 1–4.30pm; admission charge; metro: Malostranská; map p.132 B2

The Loreta church in Prague was founded by Kateřina of Lobkovic in 1626. It was built to house a replica of the 'Santa Casa' (Holy House) of the Loreta church in Rome. The Santa Casa in the centre of the Prague Loreta's courtyard was designed by Giovanni Battista Orsi and built 1626–31.

Unlike the simple original, the shrine became, across the centuries, an entire complex consisting of various buildings with several chapels, ornate cloisters and the Church of the Nativity. Dominating the group is the early Baroque tower, built in 1694, which has a carillon that rings out every hour.

Just as in the Rome Loreta, the shrine's outer walls are decorated with Renaissance reliefs. The interior also follows the Italian model and inside the small, bare building – probably the copy of a house in Palestine – is the Loreta Madonna which is worshipped by Catholic pilgrims.

The two-storey cloisters surrounding two courtyards were enlarged by the Bavarian Baroque architect Kilián Ignaz Dientzenhofer in 1740. The paintings in these cloisters have perhaps been a little over-restored. However, the poetic – and at times amusing – images of the supplications to Mary are worth craning your neck up to see.

Between the entrance and the Santa Casa you can see the **Church of the Nativity** *(Kostel Narození Pánů)*, with frescoes by Baroque artist Václav Vavřinec Reiner, and some macabre skeletons. The elaborately decorated church was consecrated in 1737, exactly 111 years after the laying of the foundation stone.

St Vitus's Cathedral (Katedrála sv. Víta)

Third Courtyard; tel: 257 531 622; www.katedralapraha.cz; Mar–Oct Mon–Sat 9am–5pm, Sun noon–5pm, Nov–Feb Mon–Fri 9am–4pm, Sun noon–4pm; free; metro: Malostranská; map p.132 C1

The 600-year history of the building of St Vitus's Cathedral began when the archbishopric was founded in 1344. Ambitious as ever, Charles IV used this opportunity to begin the construction of a cathedral which was intended to be among the most important works of the 14th-century Gothic style that was spreading from France. To this end, Charles employed the French architect Matthew of Arras, who had trained in the French Gothic school and was working in Avignon (at that time a papal city). Matthew died after eight years and the work was taken over by Petr Parléř, who influenced all later Gothic architecture in Prague.

After Parléř's death, his sons continued the work, giving the building their own individual stamp, until construction was interrupted in the first half of the 15th century by the Hussite Wars. It was in this period that the choir, its chapels and part of the south tower were completed. Only a few alterations were made during the years that followed. For instance, the top of the tower was given a Renaissance look sometime after 1560. This was replaced by a Baroque roof some 200 years later.

THE EXTERIOR

The **Rose Window**, more than 10m (33ft) in diameter, portrays the creation of the world. On either side of the

> The task of completing St Vitus's was not attempted until the 1860s, when a Czech patriotic association took it up. Following old plans and consulting Czech artists, they completed the building in 1929. The additions carried out across the centuries explain why the cathedral lacks a certain unity of style.

> The Loreta's main attraction is the **Treasure Chamber**. As in other places of pilgrimage, over the years votive gifts have been given to the treasury. The gifts of the Bohemian nobility were commissioned from notable goldsmiths of the time and include some of the most valuable works of liturgical art in Central Europe. The most remarkable is the diamond monstrance, which was a legacy of Ludmilla Eva Franziska of Kolowrat. The monstrance, made in 1699 by Baptist Kanischbauer and Matthias Stegner of Vienna to a design by Johann Bernard Fischer von Erlach, is studded with 6,222 diamonds.

window are carved portraits of the cathedral architects. The towers are decorated with the statues of 14 saints. Below, the cathedral's bronze doorways have reliefs in bronze depicting (centre door) the history of the building and (left and right) the legends of St Adalbert and St Wenceslas, including the murder of the latter by his brother.

The **Golden Gate** (*Zlatá brána*) is the distinctive portal that leads into the south transept. It is the ceremonial entrance to the cathedral, and it was through here that monarchs passed on their way to their coronation. Its remarkable triple-arched anteroom has an exterior mosaic depicting the Last Judgement and made by Italian artists in around 1370. The anteroom itself is fitted with a grille illustrating the months of the year.

THE INTERIOR

In the splendid interior of the cathedral the most notable features are the stained-glass windows and the **Triforium**, a walkway above the pillars with a gallery of portrait busts. Leading Czech artists took part in creating the windows, among them Max Švabinský, who was responsible for the window in the first chapel on the right, the mosaic on the west wall and the great window above the south portal. The window in the third chapel on the left was designed by Alfons Mucha. However, all 21 of the chapels contain several notable works of art.

The main attraction inside the generally overcrowded cathedral is **St Wenceslas's Chapel** (*Kaple sv. Václava*), which protrudes into the south transept (entry to the chapel is not possible; it must be viewed from its doorways). It was built by Petr Parléř on the site of a 10th-century Romanesque rotunda, in which the national saint Wenceslas was interred. In keeping with the importance of the Wenceslas cult, the saint's sacred place is exceptionally ornate.

The wall frescoes, which are decorated with semi-precious stones and gold, portray (in the upper half) Christ's passion and (in the lower) the story of St Wenceslas. A little door leads to the **Treasure Chamber** directly above the chapel.

Here the Bohemian royal regalia are kept, behind seven locks, the seven keys of which are held by seven separate institutions.

The three central chapels of the choir, behind the main altar, contain the Gothic tombs of the princes and kings of the Přemyslid dynasty, and are the work of Petr Parléř's masons. In the choir itself, on the left side is a kneeling bronze statue of Cardinal von Schwarzenberg, by Josef Myslbek. On the right-hand side of the choir is the ostentatious silver tomb of the 17th-century cleric St John Nepomuk, designed by the Baroque architect Johann Emanuel Fischer von Erlach. Also remarkable are the Baroque wooden reliefs in the choir showing the city of Prague. Beyond the tomb of St Nepomuk is the extraordinary late Gothic **Royal Oratory**. The balcony is supported by a fantastic complex of intertwined foliage. The organ loft originally marked the end of the choir on the west side. Once the neo-Gothic part of the cathedral was completed, however, it was moved to its present position.

Opposite the tomb of Count Schlick, designed by Matthias Bernard Braun, a staircase leads down into the **Royal Crypt** (closed at

present for 'technical reasons'). Here you can see the remains of the walls of two Romanesque churches that previously stood on the site of the cathedral, as well as the sarcophagi of Charles IV, his children and his four wives, George of Poděbrady and other rulers. Emperor Rudolf II lies in a Renaissance pewter coffin. Sitting above the Royal Crypt – just in front of the neo-Gothic high altar – is the impressive white marble imperial tomb of the Habsburgs, built for Ferdinand I, his wife Anna and their son Maximilian.

On the southern side of the neo-Gothic nave is the entry to the **Great South Tower** (like the crypt, currently closed for 'technical reasons'). The views from the top are stupendous and give a fascinating view of the cathedral's roofs and buttresses; beware, however, of the narrow, spiral staircase with its 287 steps. In the room at the top is a clock made for Rudolf II in 1597.

Strahov Monastery (Strahovský klášter)
Strahovský nádvoří 1; tel: 233 107 749; www.strahovsky klaster.cz; daily 9am–noon, 1–5pm; admission charge; tram: 22, 23; map p.132 A2–B2
The Strahov complex sits on the slopes of Petřín Hill. The

> On the corner of Karoliny Světlé and Konviktská in Staré Město lies the **Rotunda of the Holy Cross** (*Rotunda sv. Kříže*; closed to the public), a small Romanesque round church dating from the beginning of the 12th century and restored during the late 19th century.

first monastery of the district monks of the Premonstratensian Order was founded in 1140 by King Vladislav II, but was completely destroyed by fire in 1258. Very little remains of the original Romanesque building, and today the monastery is predominantly Baroque in style, although it contains early Gothic and Renaissance elements. Only St Mary's Church retains visible traces of the Romanesque original.

The monastery continued to function until 1952. After the dissolution of all religious orders in Czechoslovakia under the communist regime, it was declared a museum of literature. The monastery complex was returned to the Order with the downfall of the communist government in 1989, and the Premonstratensian monks are back in charge.

On the left as you enter Strahovské náměstí, the square around which the monastery complex is built, is

St Rochus's Church *(chrám sv. Rocha)*, built 1603–12 during the rule of Emperor Rudolf II, and now used as a gallery.

Across the square, **St Mary's Church** *(Nanebevzetí Panny Marie)*, next door to the monastery, is usually closed to the public, although the interior can be seen through a grille in the porch. This impressive Romanesque building was vastly altered and richly redecorated in the Baroque style during the 17th and 18th centuries. Much of the decorative work by Czech artist Jiří Neunhertz depicts scenes from the life of St Norbert, Archbishop of Magdeburg and founder of the Premonstratensian Order in northern France in 1120. It is believed that his remains were brought to this church during the 17th century. The church's organ was once played by Mozart.

THE STRAHOV LIBRARY
The monastery possesses one of the oldest, most extensive and most valuable libraries in the country. The collection was established at the time of the monastery's foundation over 800 years ago. One of the most famous of all the manuscripts is the **Strahov Gospels**, the oldest manuscript in the library, dating from the 9th–10th centuries.

The monastery's greatest attractions are these two library halls, the entrance to which is on the southern side of the square, by the Church of St Mary. The first of these is the Filozofický sál (Philosophical Hall), built by Ignaz Palliardi from 1782–4. The Rococo ceiling fresco (1794)

Left: details at St Vitus's and Strahov.

Right: the Strahov Gospels.

is the work of Franz Anton Maulbertsch and shows the development of humanity through wisdom.

The Teologický sál (Theological Hall) next door was built by Giovanni Domenico Orsi in 1671–9 in a rich Baroque style at a cost of 2,254 guilders. It was painted with splendid ceiling frescoes by Siardus Nosecký, a member of the Order, between 1723 and 1727. Its theme is wisdom through the knowledge of God. In the middle of the room stand a number of valuable astronomical globes from the Netherlands, dating from the 17th century.

The closest end of the corridor linking the two library rooms is lined with display cabinets of curiosities. They are mostly specimens of marine creatures from a collection owned by Karel Jan Erben, and were acquired by the monastery in 1798. One of the more bizarre pieces is a chimera.

The cloisters of the monastery now contain the **Strahov Collection of Art**.
SEE ALSO MUSEUMS AND GALLERIES, P.86

Staré Město

Bethlehem Chapel (Betlémská kaple)
Betlémské náměstí; tel: 224 248 595; www.suz.cvut.cz; Apr–Oct Tue–Sun 10am–6.30pm, Nov–Mar 10am–5.30pm; admission charge; metro: Národní Třída; map p.134 A3

St Giles's Church (Kostel sv. Jiří) on Husova has a splendid Gothic exterior (built in the mid-14th century), which contrasts with the ornate Baroque interior, decorated with paintings by Václav Vavřinec Reiner.

In Betlémské náměstí is an important Hussite memorial, the Bethlehem Chapel. It was here that mass was first said in Czech instead of Latin. The plain interior, which could hold up to 3,000 people, had the pulpit as its focal point and not the altar. The building dates from 1391; it was here that Jan Hus preached from 1402 until shortly before his martyrdom at Constance in 1415. So, too, did Thomas Münzer, the leader of the German peasants' revolt, a century later, in 1521. Taken over by the Jesuits in the 17th century, after Protestantism was banned, the chapel was rebuilt, but then demolished in 1786. It was meticulously reconstructed in its original form in 1950–4, partly making use of original building materials. In the adjoining rooms there is a small display on the life of Jan Hus.

Cathedral of Our Lady Before Týn (Chram Matky Boží před Týnem)
Staromestské náměstí; tel: 222 318 186; www.tynska. farnost.cz; July–Aug: Mon–Fri 9am–noon, 1–2pm; free; metro: Staroměstská; map p.134 B3
Our Lady Before Týn Church is a source of national pride to the Czechs, and the façade, particularly when floodlit at night, is one of the finest sights in the Old Town. Built in 1365, it was the third

church to occupy this site, the successor to Romanesque and early-Gothic buildings.

George of Poděbrady (1458–71) had a gold chalice set into the gable niche between the church's two towers as a symbol of the Hussite faith and until 1621 this was the main church of the Hussites. When the Catholic Habsburgs took over during the 1620s it was replaced by a statue of the Virgin; the chalice was melted down to make her crown, halo and sceptre.

If the church is shut – the opening times change regularly – you can usually see the interior from the glass partition in the porch. The paintings on the high altar and on the side altars are by Karel Škréta, the founder of Bohemian Baroque painting; the tall nave was given Baroque vaulting after a fire. Other remarkable works of art are the Gothic Madonna (north aisle), the Gothic pulpit and the oldest remaining font in Prague (1414). To the right of the high altar is the tombstone of the famous Danish astronomer Tycho Brahe (1546–1601), who worked at the court of Rudolf II.

The window immediately to the right of the southern door is a curiosity; through it you can see into the church from the neighbouring

47

house. One resident who had this privilege was Franz Kafka.

Church of St Francis (Kostel sv. Františka)

Křižovnické náměstí; tel: 222 329 532; open for services and concerts; metro: Staroměsstká; map p.134 A3

By the Charles Bridge is the Baroque Church of St Francis. The Knights of the Cross, after whom the square is named, were founded as a Crusader order of monks in the early 13th century. The domed church was designed by the French architect Jean-Baptiste Mathey.

Church of St James (Kostel sv. Jakuba)

Malá štupartská; Mon–Sat 9.30am–noon, 2–4pm, Sun 2–4pm; free; metro: Staroměstská; map p.134 B2

Like so many churches in Prague, St James's was originally founded by the Minorites during the reign of Charles IV, and was rebuilt several times until it attained its present Baroque form. Notable works of art are the reliefs on the main entrance, the ceiling frescoes and the painting by Václav Vavřinec Reiner on the high altar. Particularly important is the tomb of Count Vratislav Mitrovic, the work of Johann Bernhard Fischer von Erlach and Ferdinand Brokoff.

A more gruesome feature is the 400-year-old decomposed arm hanging on the west wall, supposedly amputated from a thief who tried to steal the jewels from the altar, but who was stopped, legend has it, by the Madonna grabbing his offending arm. The almost theatrical quality of the interior provides a fine stage for the frequent organ concerts given on the ornamental and powerful instrument dating from 1705.

Church of St Martin-in-the-Wall (Sv. Martin ve zdi)

Martinská 8; tel: 604 759 062; www.martinvezdi.cz; open for services only, Sun 10.30am; metro: Národní Třída; map p.134 B4

Originally Romanesque, later rebuilt in Gothic style, St Martin-in-the-Wall was, as the name suggests, incorporated into the city walls. Here, in 1414, Holy Communion was first administered 'in both forms' (ie both bread and wine given to the laity).

St Nicholas's Church (Kostel sv. Mikuláše)

Staroměstské náměstí; tel: 224 190 991; www.svmikulas.cz; Tue, Thur–Fri 10am–noon, Wed 2–4pm; free; metro: Staroměstská; map p.134 B3

The beautiful white Baroque façade of St Nicholas's Church is the work of Kilián Ignaz Dientzenhofer, built between 1732 and 1735 on the site of an earlier 13th–14th-century building. The dark statues on the outside are by Anton Braun, a nephew of Matthias Bernhard Braun. The unusual proportions of the church have come about because houses originally stood in front of the building, completely separating it from the square. However, the sparse interior is somewhat disappointing in comparison, having suffered at the hands of Emperor Josef II, who ordered the site to be used as a storage warehouse.

St Saviour's Church (Kostel sv. Salvátora)

Křižovnické náměstí; tel: 222 220 879; daily 10am–6pm; free; metro: Staroměsstká; map p.134 B2

St Saviour's Church with its Baroque façade is part of the Jesuit college, the Clementinum. This broad complex was founded by the Jesuits, who were called to Prague in 1556 to help coax the country back into the Catholic fold. But in 1773, not long after the building was completed, the Jesuits were exiled from the

Left: Emmaus Monastery.

country. The church was built 1578–1601, and the interior is notable for its ceiling painting by K. Kovář.

Nové Město

Church of Our Lady of the Snows (Kostel Panny Marie Sněžné)

Jungmannovo náměstí 18; tel: 224 490 350; www.pms.ofm.cz; Mon–Sat 9am–3pm; free; metro: Národní Třída; map p.134 B4

The Gothic Church of Our Lady of the Snows was planned as a huge building in the 14th century. Today, all that is visible is the choir. Our Lady of the Snows was planned as a coronation church by Charles IV in 1347, and the designs envisaged a three-aisled Gothic cathedral church, comparable to St Vitus's (see p.44), and which was to be the tallest building in Prague. However, shortage of money and the start of the Hussite Wars saw to it that the plans were never fulfilled. This is why the proportions of the church look rather odd, although the height of the interior is impressive. Inside, the 16th-century altar and the font dating from 1459 are worth special attention.

On 17 May 1942 two parachutists sent from Britain by the Czechoslovak government in exile succeeded in assassinating Reinhard Heydrich, the brutal Nazi governor (Reichsprotektor) of Bohemia and Moravia. After the murder, the assassins and five other members of the resistance movement barricaded themselves into the crypt of SS Cyril and Methodius. Their hiding place was discovered on 18 June, and they shot themselves rather than surrender to the SS.

Church of St Ignatius (Kostel sv. Ignáce)

Ječná 2; tel: 221 990 200; www.jesuit.cz; open for Mass; metro: Karlovo náměstí; map p.136 B2

In the middle of Charles Square is the Baroque Church of St Ignatius. This is where the Jesuits built their second college after the Clementinum in 1659. The college was dissolved in 1770 and since then the large complex has served as a hospital. The church, which was built between 1665 and 1670 by Carlo Lurago, was extended in 1679–99, with a pillared hall and arcade designed by Paul Ignaz Bayer. Inside, among other works of art, is a beautiful altarpiece depicting Christ in prison by Karel Škréta (1610–74).

Church of St John on the Rock (Kostel sv. Jana na Skalce)

Vyšehradská; closed to the public; metro: Karlovo náměstí; map p.136 B2

Almost directly opposite the Emmaus Monastery is the towering façade of the Church of St John on the Rock. This beautiful Baroque church was designed by Kilián Ignaz Dientzenhofer and built 1729–39. The restricted access is unfortunate, as inside there are some notable works of art, including a wonderful ceiling fresco of St John Nepomuk (1745), and a wooden statue by Jan Brokoff.

Church of SS Cyril and Methodius (Kostel sv. Cyrila a Metoděje)

Resslova/Na Zderaze; tel: 224 916 100; www.pravoslavna cirkev.cz; exhibition Tue–Sun Mar–Oct 10am–5pm, Nov–Feb 10am–4pm; admission charge; metro: Karlovo Náměstí; map p.136 A2

The Church of SS Cyril and

On Na slupi in Nové Město is an important (but often locked) church, Zvestovaní Panny Marie na slupi. This former convent church of the nuns of the Elizabethan Order is a rare example of a Gothic church supported by a central pillar.

Methodius is now best known for its part in the tragic history of World War II resistance (see box, below left). The church is usually closed, but you can see through the windows in the porch into the ornate Baroque interior. Below, in the crypt is the **National Memorial to the Heroes of the Heydrich Terror** (Národního památníku hrdinů heydrichády, see box left).

Church of the Virgin Mary and Charlemagne (Kostel Panny Marie a sv. Karla Velikého)

Horská; Sun 2–4.30pm; free; metro: I.P. Pavlova; map p.136 C3

The Church of the Virgin Mary and Charlemagne, the former Augustinian Karlov Monastery, is surrounded by university buildings. It is evident just by looking at the exterior that it is an unusual building, having an octagonal ground plan and a central dome. Founded in 1350 by Charles IV and dedicated to Charlemagne in 1377, it is reminiscent of the imposing Imperial Chapel in Aachen in Germany. Although the basic plan is much earlier, the spectacular roof of the nave dates from the 16th century, while below, in the crypt, is a fake grotto dating from the 18th century.

Emmaus Monastery (Klášter na Slovanech)

Vyšehradská 49; tel: 221 979 211; www.emauzy.cz; Mon–Fri 9am–5pm, Sat 11am–5pm; admission charge; metro: Karlovo náměstí; map p.136 A3

The Slavonic Monastery, also called the Emmaus (Emauzy) Monastery, was founded by Charles IV in 1347 for Croatian Benedictines, and it became most famous as a medieval scriptorium producing Slavonic manuscripts. Like many churches in Prague, it was given Baroque towers in 1635, but in 1880 was stripped of these elements and returned to something approaching its original Gothic appearance. However, this was not to last for long, as much of the building was destroyed by an Allied bombing raid in 1945.

Reconstruction and restoration began in the 1950s and, while much of it is now finished, is still ongoing. To replace the towers, two concrete sail-shaped buttresses were added in 1965–8, designed by František Černý.

In the cloisters is a series of Gothic frescoes dating from the 14th century. Many are damaged from the bombing, but what remains is still colourful. Notable are the *Flight into Egypt* and the series of saints climbing a ladder to heaven. Just off the cloisters is the highly ornate Imperial Chapel, while close by is the entrance to the light and airy space of the reconstructed church, which still retains some original decoration.

St Catherine's Church (Kostel sv. Kateřiny)

Kateřinská 30; closed to the public; metro: I.P. Pavlova; map p.136 B2

St Catherine's Church goes back to a foundation laid by Charles IV in 1355, but was largely destroyed during the Hussite Wars in the 15th century. The octagonal Gothic tower is all that remains of the medieval building. The present-day church is the result of work undertaken in 1737.

St Ursula's Church (Kostel sv. Voršily)

Národní Třída; open for Mass, Sun 11am; metro: Národní Třída; map p.136 A1

The Baroque Ursuline Convent and St Ursula's Church date from 1672 and were designed by Marco Antonio Canevalle. The church has been restored, and in front of it is a group of statues. Best-known is St John Nepomuk surrounded by cherubs, by Ignaz Platzer, dating from 1746–7.

Vyšehrad

Church of SS Peter and Paul (Kostel sv. Petra a Pavla)

K rotundě; tel: 224 911 353; www.praha-vysehrad.cz; Wed–Mon 9am–noon, 1–5pm; free; metro: Vyšehrad; map p.136 A4

The vast, neo-Gothic, twin-spired Church of SS Peter and Paul dates from the mid-1880s. Archaeologists have been kept busy examining the walls of its predecessors on the same site, as there has been a church here since the 11th century, which was destroyed by fire in the 13th century. Vyšehrad used to be a place of pilgrimage, and here, in this sandstone church, the votive tablet popularly known as the Madonna of the Rains was kept, along with the tomb of St Longinus.

St Martin's Rotunda (Rotunda sv. Martina)

V pevnosti; tel: 241 410 348; www.praha-vysehrad.cz; entry only by prior arrangement; metro: Vyšehrad; map p.136 B4

The oldest building in Vyšehrad is St Martin's Rotunda, a tiny Romanesque church dating from the 11th century, sensitively restored in the 1870s, and one of the oldest churches in the country.

Holešovice

Church of St Anthony (Kostel Sv. Antonína)

Strossmayerovo náměstí; Mon–Fri 7am–6.15pm, Sat 7–9am, 5–6.15pm, Sun 7am–noon, 5–6.15pm; free; metro: Holešovice

The church of St Anthony was built in 1908–14. The towers are clearly derived from those on the Týn Church in Staré Město. Inside is an imposing altar surrounded by a well-executed frieze, and elegant plain columns along the nave that sprout into the neo-Gothic vaulting. As well as some good *fin de siècle* stained glass, there is also an interesting fake grotto, dripping with stalactites.

Břevnov

Břevnov Monastery (Břevnovský kláster)

Markétská 1; tel: 220 406 111; www.brevnov.cz; guided tours

Left: Church of the Sacred Heart.

Left: Hussite Cathedral.

Sat–Sun Apr–Oct 10am, 2 and 4pm, Nov–Mar 10am, 2pm; tram: 15, 22, 25
The Břevnov Monastery is the oldest in Prague, founded in 993 by Boleslav II and St Adalbert; its present Baroque appearance dates from the early 18th century. The most interesting part of the complex is the **Church of St Margaret** (Bazilika svaté Markéty; Mon–Sat 7am–6pm).

This beautifully renovated church was remodelled in 1708–45 by Christoph Dienzenhofer and Kilián Ignaz. Most of the altar paintings are by Petr Brandl, while the ceiling was painted in 1719–21 by Jan Jakub Steinfels. Under the choir is an 11th-century pre-Romanesque crypt. Note the early carving preserved on the outside of the church.

Church of Our Lady of Victory (Panny Marie Vítežné na Bílé hoře)
Karlovarská 3; closed to the public; tram: 22, 25
The attractive Church of Our Lady of Victory is close to the tram terminus at Bílá Hora. This early Baroque building – erected in 1713 to commemorate the Catholic victory in 1620 – was designed by Czech architect Jan Blažej Santini. The dome frescoes by Cosmas Damian Asam, Johann Adam Schöpf and Wenzl Lorenz Reiner are worth a look.

Vinohrady

Church of St Ludmilla (Svatá Ludmila)
Jugoslávská 27; tel: 222 521 558; www.ok.cz/ludmila; open for services; metro: Náměstí Míru
At the centre of náměstí Míru is the large neo-Gothic church of St Ludmilla. Built 1888–93 and designed by Josef Mocker, it has some interesting stained glass as well as carvings by Josef Myslbek. (As with a number of other Prague churches it is not often open, but you can see the interior through the glass in the porch).

Church of St Wenceslas (Kostel Sv. Václav)
Náměstí Svatopluka Čecha; open for services; tram: 4, 22, 34
Josef Gočár and Alois Wachsman's Church of St Wenceslas (1929–30) is actually in the district of Vršovice, just to the south of Vinohrady. The striking building is set into the contour of the hill, and the high central tower makes a dramatic statement, while the interior is light and airy, cleverly lit by a series of stained-glass windows on a series of terraced roofs.

Church of the Sacred Heart (Nejsvětějšího Srdce Páně)
Náměstí Jiřího z Poděbrad; tel: 221 714 444; open for services; metro: Jiřího z Poděbrad
The Church of the Sacred Heart on náměstí Jiřího z Poděbrad is the most unusual Modernist building in Prague. Designed by the architect Josip Plečnik (who was responsible for the restoration of St Vitus's), it was built in 1928–32, early considering its eclectic style that looks forward to the later developments of post-modernism. The monolithic structure uses elements of classical and Egyptian styles on what is a rather uncompromising exterior, impressive but in some ways hard to like. However, it is enlivened by the huge glass clock on the narrow tower flanked by obelisks.

The interior (unfortunately often closed to visitors) is, unlike the forbidding façade, high and spacious, with a coffered ceiling. The tower is climbed via a ramp to the clock – double-sided so the light streams through from one side of the tower to the other – and peering out through the glass faces gives a spectacular view over the city.

Hussite Cathedral (Husův sbor)
Dykova; open for services; metro: náměstí Míru
Pavel Janák's Hussite congregational building is reached from náměstí Míru along Korunní and then by turning right down Kladská. Built 1931–3, the building is designed with both living quarters and a prayer hall. Perhaps of most interest to visitors will be the monument on the northern side that commemorates the use of the tower by Czech resistance fighters as the site of a radio transmitter during World War II.

Cinema

Czech films still attract the crowds in Prague, even though local filmmakers struggle to make ends meet. The Velvet Generation of filmmakers are responsible for hits such as *Kolya* (Jan Sverák, 1996), *Divided We Fall* (Jan Hrebejk, 2000) and *Something Like Happiness* (Bohdan Sláma, 2005). Such popular Czech films are sometimes shown with English subtitles *(s anglickými titulky)*, while foreign films are usually screened with the original soundtrack and Czech subtitles *(s českými titulky* or *č t* for short). For cinema listings, see the *Prague Post* (www.praguepost.cz) or the monthly *Culture in Prague* (www.ceskakultura.cz/praha-kina).

Cinemas

Aero
Biskupcova 31, Žižkov; tel: 271 771 349, reservations: 608 330 088; www.kinoaero.cz; tram: 1, 9, 16; metro: Želivského
Shows seasons and retrospectives of art cinema from around the world. Bar open daily from 4pm until midnight.

Blaník
Václavské náměstí 56; tel: 224 032 172; www.divadloblanik.cz; tram: 11, metro: Muzeum; map p.134 C4
Newly renovated auditorium showing reruns of recent films as well as staging live theatre.

Evald
Národní 28; tel: 221 105 225; www.cinemart.cz; tram: 6, 9, 18, 22, metro: Národní Třída; map p.134 B4
Small 72-seat art-house cinema run by film distribution company CinemArt.

French Institute
Štěpánská 35; tel: 221 401 011; www.ifp.cz; tram: 3, 9, 14, 24, metro: Můstek; map p.134 B4
The Institute's own cinema ('Kino 35') shows films from France and elsewhere in their original language with subtitles (usually Czech, though sometimes English). Tickets are very inexpensive.

Lucerna
Vodičkova 36; tel: 224 216 972; www.lucerna.cz; tram: 3, 9, 14, 24, metro: Můstek; map p.134 B4
Situated in the Lucerna shopping arcade, this gorgeous Belle Epoque cinema was opened in 1909 (commissioned by Václav Havel's grandfather). It plays a mixture of the artier Hollywood features and independent films.

Left: Aero cinema shows art house hits.

Since the late 1990s, Prague has become a popular filming location for Hollywood blockbusters. A combination of the city's architecture, relatively low costs and the existing motion-picture infrastructure at the **Barrandov Studios** (in the south of Prague) have proved attractive to production companies, who have come here to make such blockbusters as *Mission Impossible* (1996), *The Bourne Identity* (2002) and *Casino Royale* (2006).

MAT Studio
Karlovo náměstí 19; tel: 224 915 765; www.mat.cz; tram: 3, 4, 6, 14, 16, 18, 22, 24, metro: Karlovo Náměstí; map p.136 A2
Tiny cinema screening Czech features and documentaries, often with English subtitles.

Ponrepo
Bio Konvikt Theatre, Bartolomějská 13; tel: 224 233 281; www.nfa.cz; tram: 6, 9, 18, 22, metro: Národní Třída; map p.134 A4
This is the cinema of the Czech Film Archive. Before you can see a film you have to fill in a form for a member-

Left: *Kolya*, one of many hits from the Velvet Generation.

Febiofest
Late Mar; venues: Village Cinemas Anděl and Ponrepo – see above; tel: 221 101 111; www.febiofest.cz
Largest film festival in Prague, showing over 250 films from all over the world, some with English subtitles.

French Film Festival
Late Nov; French Institute – see above; tel: 221 401 011; www.ifp.cz
Some of the films are introduced by French actors and directors.

Karlovy Vary International Film Festival
Early July; various venues; tel: 221 411 011; www.kviff.com
Main event is at the Hotel Thermal in the spa town of Karlovy Vary, but cinemas in Prague also take part. Showcases Hollywood blockbusters as well as some indie films, with famous actors and directors in attendance.

One World Human Rights Film Festival
Late Apr; various venues; tel: 739 320 639; www.oneworld.cz
Documentaries and features on human rights themes shown at Aero, the Evald and Lucerna among other venues. Many films are in English or have English subtitles.

ship card (available Mon–Fri 3–6pm). Photo ID is required. The beautiful screening room shows Czech and Slovak films as well as classics of world cinema. Some films are (inconveniently for non-Czechs) given a live spoken Czech translation (denoted by '*spřekl*' on the programme) during the film.

MULTIPLEXES
Cinema City Flora
Vinohradská 149; tel: 255 742 021; www.cinemacity.cz; tram: 11, metro: Flora
IMAX cinema located in the Palác Flora shopping mall.

Palace Cinemas – Nový Smíchov
Plzeňská 8; tel: 257 181 212; www.palacecinemas.cz; tram: 4, 6, 7, 9, 10, 12, 14, 20, metro: Anděl
Twelve-screen cinema located within a shopping mall.

Village Cinemas Anděl City
Radlická 3179; tel: 251 115 111; www.villagecinemas.cz; tram: 4, 6, 7, 9, 10, 12, 14, 20, metro: Anděl

New 12-screen cinema with luxury seating and high-quality sound system.

Film Festivals
Days of European Film
Apr; main venue: Aero – see above; tel: 604 607 477; www.eurofilmfest.cz
Two-week festival showing films from the EU (many films have English subtitles). Festival includes a couple of quadruple-bills for the true cineaste.

Right: festival at Kino Aero.

A New Wave of Czech cinema occurred from 1963 to 1968, achieving international acclaim. Films such as *Closely Watched Trains* (Jiří Menzel) and *The Shop on Main Street* (Klos and Ján Kadár) won Oscars, and Miloš Forman's *The Firemen's Ball* and *Loves of a Blonde* were nominated. After the Soviet clampdown in 1968, many directors chose to emigrate and established themselves abroad.

Essentials

Prague is an easy city to negotiate for tourists, as is fitting for a place that receives such a high number of foreign visitors. The Czechs are generally friendly and willing to help out with directions if you get lost and do not seem to mind the regular influx of travellers. What they have taken exception to, however, are the stag- and hen-parties that have used the city as a living venue for over-the-top revelry. The city is trying to throw off this image, and the recent rise in prices for foreign visitors has gone some way to alleviating the problem.

Climate

Prague generally has a mild version of the standard Central European climate, cold winters and warm summers. So generally you want plenty of warm clothes for the winter, including gloves and a hat, and light clothes for the summer. However, the weather can be changeable, so it is advisable always to have a light jumper or coat with you in the summer, and to carry an umbrella. If you intend to visit churches then you should be modestly dressed with covered shoulders and no shorts or short skirts to avoid giving offence.

Disabled Travellers

Prague's public transport was not designed with disabled people in mind. Most metro stations and all trams and buses involve climbing and descending what can be very steep steps. In addition, pavement kerbs do not often have ramps. But in general Praguers take a courteous view towards people with disabilities, and will make efforts to assist them.

Emergencies

General emergency tel: 112
Ambulance tel: 155
Fire Brigade tel: 150
Police tel: 158

Embassies and Consulates

Australia: Klimentská 10; Prague 1; tel: 296 578 350
Canada: Muchova 6, Prague 6; tel: 272 101 800; www.canada.cz
Ireland: Tržiště 13, Prague 1; tel: 257 530 061
New Zealand: Dykova 19, Prague 1; tel: 222 514 672
South Africa: Ruská 65, Prague 10; tel: 267 311 114
United Kingdom: Thunovská 14, Prague 1; tel: 257 402 111; www.britain.cz
United States: Tržiště 15, Prague 1; tel: 257 022 000; www.usembassy.cz

Gay and Lesbian Travellers

Generally gay and lesbian travellers will encounter few difficulties in Prague, although very public displays of attention may attract stares. The age of consent for heterosexuals, gays and lesbians is 15.
SEE ALSO NIGHTLIFE, P.104

Health

Visiting the Czech Republic poses no major health concerns, and you do not need inoculations. Citizens of EU countries are entitled to free emergency treatment. Make sure you have your European Health Insurance Card before travelling. You will be charged for any further treatment, so it still makes sense to take out health insurance. For minor health problems Prague has modern pharmacies (look for a green cross, or the word *lékárna* on the front of the shop), including 24-hour facilities at Štefánikova 6 and Palackého 5.

Media

Press

All the main foreign-language newspapers are available at newsstands in the city. The *Prague Post* (www.praguepost. com), published weekly in English, contains news and comment as well as events listings, as does the bi-

Mobile Phones

Most people will find that their own mobile phone will work in Prague (even if the charges will be much higher than using phonecards). However, for longer stays it is better and much cheaper to buy one of the easily available local pay-as-you-go SIM cards. The main companies are O2 (www.cz.o2.com) and Vodafone (www.vodafone.cz).

Time Zone

Prague operates on Central European Time (CET). This is one hour ahead of GMT in winter and two hours ahead of GMT in summer.

Tipping

Tipping levels are low, and in some restaurants service is included in the price.

Tourist Information

The **Prague Information Service** (PIS; Staroměstské náměstí; tel: 12 444; www.pis.cz) can provide much useful information, including city maps and addresses. As well as at the main address above, branches of the PIS can be found at: Na příkopě 20; the Main Station; and in the Malostranská mostecká vez in Malá Strana.

---

monthly *Prague in Your Pocket*.

Television and Radio

Satellite television has one or more English-speaking news channels. The main ones are CNN and BBC 24. Foreign broadcasts on Czech TV are dubbed rather than subtitled, although there may be English-speaking programmes on other foreign-service TV stations. Radio Praha broadcasts news in English three times each day on 101.1 FM (www.radio.cz).

Money

The currency of the Czech Republic is the crown or *koruna* (Kč). Each crown is made up of 100 hellers.

Banks open 8am–4pm, but many close at lunchtime. Most charge a standard 1 percent commission. Bureaux de change often open until 10pm, but can charge up to 30 percent commission. There are a large number of cashpoints that will issue cash against your current-account card or credit card; this is generally the easiest way to get money.

Credit cards are increasingly accepted for payment across the city. They are now accepted by most hotels, but it is still wise to double-check.

Post

Postal services are cheap and reliable for letters and postcards. Most shops that sell postcards also sell stamps, as do many hotels. Postboxes are either orange with a side slit or orange and blue with a front flap. The main post office (open 24 hours a day) is at Jindřišská 14, just off Wenceslas Square.

Telephones

The international code for the Czech Republic is 420. The city code for Prague is 2, this is included in the nine-digit number so should not be dialled extra. Most phone numbers consist of nine digits, including the area code. You should dial the entire nine-digit number even if you are dialling within the same area code. Public telephones take phonecards *(telefonní karta)*. These can be bought at post offices or newsstands.

Public Holidays

1 Jan, Day of Recovery of the Independent Czech State; **Easter Sunday and Monday**; **1 May**, Labour Day; **8 May**, Liberation Day; **5 July**, Day of Slavonic Apostles Cyril and Methodius; **6 July**, Jan Hus Day; **28 Sept**, St Wenceslas Day and Czech Statehood Day; **17 Nov**, Struggle for Freedom and Democracy Day; **24–5 Dec**, Christmas Eve and Day; **26 Dec**, St Stephen's Day.

Festivals and Events

A visit to Prague could be planned to coincide with one of the many festivals that take place during the year. Whether you are interested in classical music, puppet theatre, bacchanalian revels or sober ceremonies marking historical events, there are plenty of events to cater to your needs. The listings below present some of the highlights, though a fuller programme of events can be found at www.pis.cz/en/prague/events. Visitors interested in film festivals should also consult the chapter on 'Cinema' *(see p.53).*

January

Anniversary of Jan Palach's Protest
Commemoration of the student who set himself on fire on 16 January 1969 in protest against Soviet occupation. People gather at his memorial near St Wenceslas Statue, close to where he made his protest.

Prague Winter Festival
www.praguewinterfestival.com
A commercial venture building on the success of the spring and autumn festivals, though not generally up to the standards of the other two.

February

Masopust
www.carnevale.cz
The Czech version of Shrove Tuesday is celebrated with a five-day festival of concerts, shows and parades, mostly in the Žižkov area.

March

Opera – Musical Theatre Festival
www.divadlo.cz/jhd
A city-wide festival of musical theatre, including performances from youth theatres.

April

Burning of the Witches
A throwback to pagan times, this festival on the last day of April celebrates the end of winter, driving out its evil spirits. It is celebrated in Prague with large bonfires, usually in Kampa Park and at Výstaviště.

May

Prague Fringe Festival
See www.praguefringe.com for the packed daily roster of events.
A week-long cultural exchange in which artists from dozens of countries meet in Prague to perform everything from puppetry to classical theatre and musical cabaret.

May–June

Khamoro
www.khamoro.cz
An annual festival of Roma culture with exhibitions, music and dance.

Prague Spring
www.festival.cz
International festival of classical music, with some jazz

Left: production from Tanec Praha.

A bit of a misnomer, since this 'festival' featuring world-class performers is actually a series of concerts, usually one every couple of weeks, beginning in November and continuing until the spring.

December

St Nicholas's Eve
People gather, especially in the Old Town Square and around the Charles Bridge, on 5 December, many of them dressed as St Nicholas, an angel or a devil. Some hand out sweets to children. Others mark the occasion with a few drinks.

Christmas
The most important day for Czechs is Christmas Eve, when presents are exchanged and a feast of roast carp is eaten. During the week before, carp are sold in the street from large barrels filled with water.

New Year's Eve
Revellers gather in the Old Town Square and Wenceslas Square to let off fireworks, dance and then smash their champagne bottles.

The Czech Republic celebrates **5 July** as a national holiday. It marks the day when the Slavonic Apostles Cyril and Methodius were supposed to have arrived in 863, bringing Christianity to the country.

---

performers as well. Concerts are held at the Rudolfinum, Obecní dům and St Vitus's Cathedral.

World Festival of Puppet Art
see www.puppetart.com
A large programme of live puppetry from around the world shown at theatres around the city.

June

Prague Writers' Festival
see www.pwf.cz
This meeting of the minds draws some of the top scribes in the world. Past events have been hosted by authors Nadine Gordimer, Salman Rushdie and Gore Vidal.

Left: taking to the streets during the Prague Fringe Festival.

Tanec Praha
www.tanecpha.cz
Festival presenting a diverse programme of modern dance.

July–August

Summer Festivities of Early Music
www.collegiummarianum.cz
Festival of Renaissance and Baroque music performed on period instruments in some of the finest historic buildings in Prague.

September

Prague Autumn
www.pragueautumn.cz
A young international classical music festival, not yet on a par with Prague Spring, but with some impressive visiting performers.

October

Four Days
www.ctyridny.cz
An international festival of experimental theatre, as well as dance and music.

November

Agharta Prague Jazz Festival
www.agharta.cz

The **Struggle for Freedom and Democracy Day** is celebrated on 17 November. This is the anniversary of a student demonstration in 1939 against the Nazi occupation. A student was shot and reprisals followed, with the closing of universities and arrest and execution of more students. In 1989, students used a commemoration of the events 50 years before to protest against the communist regime. The police suppressed the demonstration, but it marked the beginning of the end.

Food and Drink

Bohemian cooking is based on the abundant produce of the country's fertile farmland, its orchards, rivers and ponds, and its vast forests teeming with game. It is unpretentious fare, intended to sustain body and soul rather than aspiring to reach the status of an art form. It can nonetheless be delicious. When it comes to drinks, there is one thing the Czechs do better than almost any other nation, and that is, of course, beer. While Pilsner is the most common type, there are many others too – dark, pale, bitter, sweet – all of them excellent. For places to eat and drink, *see also Cafés and Bars (p.30–33) and Restaurants (p.112–19).*

The Czech Diet

STAPLE FOODS

A full Czech meal *(oběd)* will normally begin with soup *(polévka)*, whether a simple meat broth *(vývar)* with dumplings, a thick potato cream soup *(bramborová)* or a bowl of tripe soup *(dršťková* – reputed to be an excellent hangover cure).

The main course is referred to half-jokingly as *vepřo-knedlo-zelo* (pork-dumpling-cabbage). Indeed, the pig is king in this country, and fortunately for visitors, is likely to be much tastier than the specimens at home. Most pigs are raised en masse, but many villagers keep a porker or two themselves. Every part is made into some tasty comestible, and the slaughter is often occasion for a *vepřové hody* (pork festival).

After pork, beef *(hovězí maso)* is the most popular meat, and is often served as *svíčková na smetaně*, fillet or sirloin topped with a slice of lemon and a spoonful of cranberries, and swimming in a cream sauce.

The usual accompaniment to meat is the dumpling *(knedlík)* – which, in fact, enjoys even more veneration than the pig. It is made from flour, bread, potatoes or semolina, with added yeast, baking powder, eggs, milk or sugar, and is prepared in a loaf-like form and then cut with a wire (never a knife).

FOWL AND GAME

If you want to move beyond *vepřo-knedlo-zelo*, richer

Left: carp is a Christmas tradition.

Left: in Prague pork is king.

than cabbage will be met with raised eyebrows. Salad (salát) is more common, probably not in the form of tossed green lettuce, but as a medley of cucumber, onion, red pepper and tomatoes wallowing in a sweetish, vinegary sauce.

DESSERT
As for dessert, options are limited. There may be thin crêpes (palačinky), wrapped around cottage cheese (tvaroh), ice cream (zmrzlina), fruit or nuts, and perhaps served with a chocolate sauce. The dumpling makes a reappearance (like it or not), this time as an ovocný knedlík, filled with plums or apricots. This is really a meal in its own right, and in Czech homes is often eaten as such.

Drinks
WINE
Winemaking in the Czech Republic is concentrated in sunny southern Moravia, where the vines spread for almost 113km (70 miles) between the city of Brno and the Austrian and Slovak borders. Among the red wines, Frankovka (relatively dry) or Sv. Vavřinec (plummy and sweetish) can be good, while white Ryzlink and Palava go well with fish.

Bohemia's vineyards cover a much smaller area, centred on the Elbe and its tributaries north of Prague. The vines growing on the steep slope below the town of Mělník are the descendants of those brought from France and planted here by Emperor Charles IV in the 14th century. They yield white wines rather like those in neighbouring Saxony, dry and rather acidic.

The environment of the Czech Republic is particularly favourable for the growth of a bewildering array of **mushrooms** (houby), a detailed knowledge of which seems part of everyone's heritage. Fungi in all shapes and sizes are hunted down and picked in favourite spots in the countryside, brought home and fried, or more likely dried, to be added later to all kinds of dishes, notably cabbage soup.

dishes include roast duck (kachna) and roast goose (husa). As well as making a celebratory meal for grand occasions, geese in the Czech Republic are also force-fed to provide husí paštíka, liver pâté as good as the finest French foie gras (irresistible, as long as you don't dwell on what the unfortunate bird has had to go through). Some restaurants will also allow you to sample the excellent variety of game reared in the fields and forests beyond Bohemia's villages. Look out for wild boar (kanec), venison (srnčí maso), pheasant (bažant) or partridge (koroptev).

FISH
Prague is the capital of a landlocked country a long way from the ocean, so Czech fish dishes depend on freshwater varieties. Roasted or fried trout (pstruh) features on many menus, but the quintessentially Czech fish is the carp (kapr), raised in their thousands in fishponds across the country. Typically netted in December, they are brought to town, sold live from barrels and kept in the family bathtub before being slaughtered and cut into steaks, breaded and fried to form the centrepiece of the traditional Christmas Eve dinner. In restaurants, carp is more likely to be served as kapr na černo, in a black, sweet-and-sour sauce made mysteriously from such ingredients as nuts, raisins, sugar, beer and vinegar.

VEGETABLES
When it comes to vegetables, a request for anything other

BEER

Although the oldest record of the brewer's art in Prague can be found in a document dating from 1082, the bottom-fermented Czech beers of today have evolved from the brew developed in the western Bohemian city of Plzeň (Pilsen) in 1842. The combination of local spring water, hops from Žatec in northern Bohemia, and cellaring in the ideal conditions of the sandstone caves beneath the city yielded a beer that won instant popularity – particularly in Germany, where its name, 'Pilsner' or 'Pils', is now indiscriminately applied to any pale, hoppy brew.

To distinguish the original product from its imitators, its makers gave it the name of 'Pilsner Urquell' meaning 'original source' (*Plzeňský prazdroj*' in Czech). Its great rival is Budějovice – known as Budweis in German and Budvar in Czech – which comes from the southern city of České Budějovice. For those who find the distinctive sharp taste of Praz-droj a little too acidic, Budvar is a somewhat sweeter, milder drink.

Brewery Visits

A century ago, there were 800 breweries in Bohemia, and every little town had at least one. Visitors wishing to tour one of the 70 or so breweries which survive today have a choice of Staropramen in Prague and Velké Popovice, about 20km (12 miles) to the southeast of the city. If you are prepared to travel further afield, your best options are Budweiser Budvar (tel: 387 705 341; www.budvar.cz) in České Budějovice, two hours south of Prague, and Pilsner Urquell (tel: 377 062 888; www.beerworld.cz) in Plzeň, one and a half hours west of Prague.

Staropramen
Nádražní 84; tel: 257 191 402; www.pivovary-staropramen.cz; guided tours daily; admission charge; tram: 6, 9, 12, 20, 58; metro: Anděl

One- or two-hour-long tours in English are offered each day, usually around lunchtime

or early afternoon, but do phone ahead to book your visit. Tours begin with a short film outlining Staropramen's history, from its construction in 1869 to its takeover by the Belgian group Interbrew (now Inbev) in 2000. Visitors then proceed to the brewhouses, where the processes of fermentation and ageing, filtration, bottling and quality control are demonstrated. The tour ends with a beer-tasting.

Velké Popovice
Ringhofferova 1, Velké Popovice; tel: 323 683 425; www.kozel.cz; daily 8am–6pm; admission charge; train from Prague's main station (Praha hlavní nádraží) to Strančice, then bus 461

This historic brewery offers tours to groups of 10 or more by prior arrangement (using the form on their website). Individuals can usually join larger groups, but all should be aware that tours in English are usually only at weekends. Tours begin with a history of

the brewery, before progressing to the new brewhouse (with its enormous copper brewing kettles), the storage cellars, the bottle- and cask-filling plant and finally the old brewhouse, where visitors can sample the end result.

Markets and Shops

Cellarius
Štěpánská 61; tel: 224 210 979; www.cellarius.cz; Mon–Sat 9.30am–9pm, Sun 3–8pm; tram: 3, 9, 14, 24, 52, 53, metro: Můstek; map p.136 B1
Located in the Lucerna shopping arcade, this wine merchant sells over 1,300 different bottles. The selection of Moravian wines is particularly good.

Fruits of France
Jindřišská 9; tel: 224 220 304; www.fdf.cz; Mon–Fri 9.30am–6.30pm, Sat 9.30am–1pm; tram: 3, 9, 14, 24, 52, 53, metro: Můstek; map p.134 C4
Opened not long after the Velvet Revolution, this upmarket greengrocer reacquainted Prague with the joys

of French produce. The shop on Jindřišská specialises in fruit, vegetables and wine, as well as an impressive array of mushrooms. A second branch at Bělehradská 94 in Vinohrady (tel: 222 511 261) offers fish, pâtés, cheese and more wine.

Havelská Market
Havelská, Staré Město; Mon–Fri 7.30am–6pm, Sat–Sun 8.30am–6pm; metro: Můstek; map p.134 B3
Nowadays, this fruit and vegetable market sells more tourist souvenirs than agricultural produce. There are, however, still a few quality greengrocers and florists left.

Pivní Galerie
U Průhonu 9; tel: 220 870 613; www.pivnigalerie.cz; Mon–Fri noon–9pm; tram: 1, 3, 5, 25
This shop sells 180 different beers from 34 breweries. You can sit down and sample a selection before you buy, and the English-speaking owner is on hand to give advice.

Robertson's
Jugoslávských partyzánů 38; tel: 233 321 142; www.robertson.cz; Mon–Fri

9am–5pm, Thur until 6.30pm, Sat 9am–1pm; tram: 8, metro: Dejvická
As the name might suggest, this shop specialises in British produce. Pride of place is given to traditional butchery – beef, bacon, lamb, sausages, etc – and indeed Robertson's supplies many of Prague's top restaurants. A large range of other products is also available, including mustards, sauces, pickles, chutney, lemon curd, marmalade, marmite, tea, cocoa, puddings and Indian sauces.

Bohemian-style **absinth** (spelt without an 'e') differs from traditional absinthe in several ways. It contains little or no anise or fennel, and has a more bitter taste owing to its higher content of absinthine. This is related to the fact that it is not produced by distillation, but rather by a simple maceration of wormwood. Czech absinthe does, however, retain the traditional quality of having a very high alcohol content.

Left: Havelská Market.

History

C.400BC
Invasion by a Celtic tribe, the Boii, from whom the name Bohemia is derived.

AD500S
Arrival of the Slavs.

900–1306
Rule of the Přemyslid dynasty; building of Prague Castle.

935
Prince Wenceslas, patron saint of Bohemia, is murdered by his brother Boleslav I.

1004
Bohemia comes definitively under the jurisdiction of the Holy Roman Empire as Jaromír of Bohemia takes Prague with the aid of a German army.

1306
King Wenceslas II is assassinated, ending the Přemyslid dynasty.

1310
King John of Luxembourg begins a new dynasty.

1348–78
Reign of King Charles I (later Emperor Charles IV, *below*); building of Charles Bridge.

1398–1415
Jan Hus preaches religious reform and is burnt at the stake.

1419
The Hussites throw Catholic councillors from a window in the New Town Hall (the first defenestration) and begin the Hussite Wars, which continue intermittently for a century.

1526
Jagiellon King Louis is killed at the Battle of Mohács in Hungary; the throne passes to the Habsburgs.

1576
Emperor Rudolf II *(right)* moves the Habsburg court to Prague.

1609
Rudolf's Letter of Majesty grants freedom of religious worship.

1618
Archduke Ferdinand tears up the Letter of Majesty. Two imperial councillors and their secretary are thrown out of a window in Hradčany (the second defenestration), providing the spark for the Thirty Years' War.

1620
Catholic victory under Emperor Ferdinand at Battle of the White Mountain. The Protestant 'Winter King', Frederick of the Palatinate, flees. Repressive measures against Protestants result in mass exile.

1680
Bohemian peasants revolt against the feudal government.

1740
War of the Austrian Succession: the armies of Bavaria, Saxony and France capture Prague. Maria Theresa becomes empress.

1757
Seven Years' War: Prussian forces bombard Prague. Maria Theresa has the castle extended and the damage to the city repaired.

1781
Josef II abolishes serfdom; Prague's Jewish citizens are awarded civic rights. The ghetto is renamed Josefov.

1787
Première of Mozart's Don Giovanni.

1845
Arrival of the railway. The Industrial Revolution draws in Czechs from the countryside, diluting the German character of the city.

1848
Nationalist revolution in Prague crushed by the Austrians.

1880S
The Czech National Theatre opens. Composers Smetana, Dvořák and Janáček gain international recognition.

1915
Tomáš Garrigue Masaryk goes into exile and gains Allied support for a new state uniting Czechs and Slovaks.

1918
Independent Republic of Czechoslovakia proclaimed. Masaryk becomes the first president, Edvard Beneš Foreign Minister.

1938
Munich Agreement cedes the Sudetenland to Hitler.

1939–45
Nazi occupation.

1945
Prague liberated by the Resistance and the Red Army. Almost all of Czechoslovakia's 2.7 million Germans are expelled.

1948
Communist coup replaces President Beneš with communist leader Klement Gottwald.

1968
Prague Spring: an attempt to introduce 'socialism with a human face' under Party Secretary General Alexander Dubček. Attempt is crushed by a Warsaw Pact invasion.

1969
Dubček dismissed and 'normalisation' – a return to strict Stalinist orthodoxy – is overseen by party leader Gustav Husák.

1989
Velvet Revolution ends the communist era. Václav Havel elected president.

1993
'Velvet Divorce' – creation of separate Czech and Slovak republics.

2002
Prague suffers severe flooding.

2003
Havel is succeeded as president by Václav Klaus.

2004
The Czech Republic joins the EU.

2006
Following inconclusive elections, the country survives seven months without a government.

2007
US proposals for locating anti-missile defences on Czech soil cause bitter controversy.

Hotels

There are some lovely places to stay in Prague, and there is a good choice of accommodation to suit all budgets. Many places are in converted Baroque – or even earlier – buildings, giving you a sense of history as well as somewhere to stay, although not all conversions are as sensitive as they might be. As a counterbalance to these older properties there are still some grand 19th-century hotels and – a more recent phenomenon – a number of chic design hotels that, while they might not give much of a sense of place, do provide a sometimes welcome relief from all the history outside.

Malá Strana

Biskupský dům

Dražického náměstí 6; tel: 257 532 320; www.hotelbishops house.com; €€–€€€; tram: 12, 22; map p.133 D2

Just off Mostecká, the 'Bishop's House' is a 19th-century building close to the Charles Bridge. The plain rooms are clean and comfortable, and quiet given the hotel's proximity to one of the city's main tourist thoroughfares.

Domus Balthazar

Mostecká 5; tel: 257 199 499; www.domus-balthasar.cz; €€; tram: 12, 22; map p.133 C2

A new design hotel in the heart of Malá Strana and admittedly well done, with modern furniture sitting well with the old beams of the rooms. It is in quite a busy location, but the hotel is very convenient for most of the

Above: Dům u velké boty.

sights in the centre of town and the rates are quite reasonable.

Dům u tří čápů

Tomášská 16; tel: 257 210 779; www.utricapu.cz; €€€; tram: 12, 22; map p.133 C2

This newly opened design hotel close to the Wallenstein Palace is excellent. Very chic, all clean lines and modern furniture, but without disturbing the original fabric of this historic building. The rooms are not only beautifully done but very central and quiet, and the café and restaurant good places to while away a few hours.

As befits one of Europe's most popular holiday destinations, demand for hotel rooms is very high in Prague, and, especially during summer when the organised tours arrive, places can get booked up very quickly and quite a long time in advance. If you have your heart set on a particular hotel make sure you book as far in advance as possible.

Dům u velké boty

Vlašská 30; tel: 257 532 088; www.dumuvelkeboty.cz; €–€€; tram: 12, 22; map p.132 B/C2

Opposite the German Embassy, this small hotel is in a superb location. The building dates from the early 17th century, and care has been taken to ensure that the interior and furniture maintain the historic feel. Lovely comfy beds, spotless bathrooms and friendly owners all go towards making this one of the best places to stay in the city. They accept cash only.

Hotel Aria

Tržiště 9; tel: 225 334 111; www.ariahotel.net; €€€€; tram: 12, 22; map p.133 C2

Price for a double room for one night without breakfast:
€ under €120
€€ €120–€180
€€€ €180–€250
€€€€ over €250

Left: Prague's smaller hotels can be cosy retreats.

of the famous Dientzenhofer family of architects, this is an interesting, secluded place to stay. The simple rooms all have attached bathrooms and are good value for the location.

Residence Nosticova
Nosticova 1; tel: 257 312 513; www.nosticova.com; €€€; tram: 12, 20, 22, 23, 57; map p.133 C3
If you have the money, this could be a delightful place to stay. The fairytale apartments are beautifully furnished (one even has a grand piano), and all have an attached bathroom and kitchen. There are large reductions for stays during low season.

U červeného lva
Nerudova 41; tel: 257 533 832; www.hotelredlion.com; €€; tram: 12, 22; map p.132 B2
A historic hotel set in a Renaissance house, previously the home of the Baroque painter Petr Brandl. The rooms have wooden floors and beautifully painted ceilings; their views aren't bad either. Under the hotel is a 14th-century cellar, now a bar.

Expensive but heavy on designer chic, this newish addition to Malá Strana plays heavily on its musical theme. From Mozart to Dizzy Gillespie, each floor and room is dedicated to a particular music or musician. The fittings and fixtures are classy, as is the in-house music library.

Hotel Neruda
Nerudova 44; tel: 257 535 557; www.hotelneruda-praha.cz; €€€; tram: 12, 22; map p.132 B2
A stone's throw away from the castle, this building dating from 1348 now has a minimalist modern interior. You are paying for the location as much as anything, but the rooms are clean and comfortable, and there is a pleasant café space where you can sit and sip hot chocolate.

Mandarin Oriental
Nebovidská 1; tel: 233 088 888; www.mandarinoriental. com; €€€€; tram: 12, 22; map p.133 C3
Cleverly inserted into the fabric of a 14th-century

monastery in the tranquil heart of Malá Strana, this luxury establishment offers superlative comfort in a historic setting. As well as individually designed bedrooms and stylish public spaces, there is a spa offering a sophisticated range of treatments.
SEE ALSO PAMPERING, P.107

Pension Dientzenhofer
Nosticova 2; tel: 257 311 319; www.dientzenhofer.cz; €€; tram: 12, 22; map p.133 D3
Set in the 16th-century home

Right: outside the Mandarin Oriental.

Zlatá hvězda

Nerudova 48; tel: 257 532 867; www.hotelgoldenstar.com; €€€; tram: 12, 22; map p.132 B2

Perched looking down Nerudova and up to the castle, the 'Golden Star' has one of the best views of any hotel in the city. Dating back to 1372, the building's interior has been preserved and restored, and this careful approach has been carried over into the rooms, with their period furniture and modern bathrooms.

Hradčany

Domus Henrici

Loretanska 11; tel: 220 511 369; www.domus-henrici.cz; €€–€€€; tram: 22, 23; map p.132 B2

Just up the hill towards the Strahov and Loreta is this lovely hotel, set in a building that (with a few alterations) dates back to the 14th century. Most of the elegant rooms have wonderful views over Malá Strana below. A good quiet location for those not keen on spending their nights in the Old Town.

Hotel Hoffmeister

Pod bruskou 7; tel: 251 017 111; www.hoffmeister.cz; €€€€; metro: Malostranská; map p.133 D1

On the corner of Chotkova as it winds up past the castle, the Hoffmeister is in a very con-

---

---

venient location. Not as attractive as some Prague hotels from the outside, but with rooms and facilities that are luxurious. Comfortable and tasteful, and with the excellent **Lily Wellness Spa** – for which it is well known – and restaurant. The prices are surprisingly good compared to some other Prague five-stars.

SEE ALSO PAMPERING, P.106

Hotel Questenberk

Úvoz 15; tel: 220 407 600; www.hotelq.cz; €€€; tram: 22, 23; map p.132 B2

With its tall Baroque façade, this converted 17th-century palace initially looks like a church. Inside, the renovation has retained enough of the original fabric to make it an atmospheric place to stay. The rather minimalist rooms do have antique furniture, and all have marble bathrooms attached.

Hotel Savoy

Keplerova 6; tel: 224 302 430; www.hotel-savoy.cz; €€€€; tram: 22, 23; map p.132 A2

The Savoy offers luxury

Right: Hotel Paříž.

rooms, admittedly well done, of the kind found in many cities across the world. Perhaps it is this international familiarity that attracts the celebs, or, possibly the stunning views across the Strahov Monastery and Petřín Hill from the Savoy and Presidential suites' balconies.

U krále karla

Nerudova/Úvoz 4; tel: 257 533 594; www.romantichotels.cz; €€–€€€; tram: 22, 23; map p.132 B2

This Baroque building (it took its present form in 1639) is in a quiet and convenient location at the top of the hill, looking out over Petřín Hill and the Strahov. The rooms lean a little more towards Central European kitsch than some, but many people will love the stained-glass windows.

U raka

Černínská 10; tel: 220 511 100; www.romantikhotel-uraka.cz; €€€; tram: 22, 23; map p.132 B1

Set in one of the only wooden houses left in Prague, and dating back to the mid-18th century, this complex is now a lovely hotel. The spotless rooms are beautifully laid out, and there is a delightful garden for the use of guests. One of the more expensive places to stay, but quiet and romantic.

Staré Město

Apostolic Residence

Saroméstéké náměstí 26; tel: 221 632 206; www.apostolic.cz; €€€; metro: Staromótská; map p.134 B3

Locations in the Old Town don't come much better than this tiny hotel. The charming rooms, with their wooden beams and period furniture, may be a little more noisy than some – on the square

Left: Hotel Josef.

and above a restaurant – but they do have a view of the Astronomical Clock.

Four Seasons Hotel
Veleslavínova 2a; tel: 221 427 000; www.fourseasons.com/prague; €€€€; tram: 17, 18, 53, metro: Staroméstská; map p.134 A3

As well as an unsurpassable location close to Charles Bridge and with views over the Vltava to Malá Strana and the castle, the Four Seasons offers all the comfort and style associated with its name. A bonus is its **Allegro** restaurant, up there with Prague's finest.
SEE ALSO RESTAURANTS, P.113

Hotel černý slon
Týnská 1; tel: 222 321 521; www.hotelcernyslon.cz; €–€€; metro: Náměstí Republiky; map p.134 B3

A lovely 14th-century building on the Unesco protected list, very close to Old Town Square. The simple but attractive rooms – those in the attic are particularly nice with their wooden beams – are excellent value, and the price includes breakfast.

Hotel Josef
Rybná 20; tel: 221 700 111; www.hoteljosef.com; €€€–€€€€; metro: Náměstí Republiky; map p.134 B2

A sleek designer hotel near the Jewish Quarter. The inte-

rior, by Eva Jiřičná, has stone-and-glass bathrooms attached to minimalist rooms with DVD and CD players. None of this is cheap (up to around 350 euros per night), but it does make a change from the often heritage-heavy accommodation available elsewhere in the city.

Hotel Paříž
Obecního domu 1; tel: 222 195 195; www.hotel-pariz.cz; €€€€; metro: Náměstí Republiky; map p.134 C3

More luxury in this squeaky-clean Art Nouveau building from 1904. Unfortunately the rooms have been rather over-restored, and the original furniture replaced with bland modern pieces that make a nod towards the original style. The **Restaurant Sarah Bernhardt** has fared rather better and retains its sparkling interior and wooden fittings.

Maximilian
Haštalská 14; tel: 225 303 111; www.maximilianhotel.com; €–€€; metro: Náměstí Republiky; map p.134 B2

This new hotel close to the Jewish Quarter and St Agnes's Convent is a bargain for both its position and the clean lines of the modern rooms. The rooms have nice little designer touches and comfortable beds, and some

have good views over the Old Town. As an added bonus the hotel also contains the **Zen City Spa**.
SEE ALSO PAMPERING, P.107

Pachtuv Palace
Karolíny Světlé 34; tel: 234 705 111; www.pachtuv palace.com; €€€€; metro: Národni třida; map p.134 A4

Convenient for the New Town and for getting across the Charles Bridge into Malá Strana, this luxury converted Baroque palace might be a good retreat for those not wishing to be in the heart of the Old Town. Some of the imaginatively converted suites have painted ceilings, and the whole effect is rather romantic.

Residence Řetězová
Řetězová 9; tel: 222 221 800; www.residenceretezova.com; €€€; metro: Staroméstská; map p.134 A3

This converted palace, just off Karlova, has nine large and comfortable apartments. Some are more luxurious than others, but all have a well-equipped kitchen and decent bathroom, and the location is excellent.

U tří bubnů
U radnice 8–10; tel: 224 214 855; www.utribubnu.cz; €€; metro: Staroméstská; map p.134 B3

The 'House at the Three

Left: Hotel Praha.

make way for comfortable, modern rooms. Its impersonable nature is offset by the luxury and excellent service.

Hotel Yasmin
Politických véz 12; tel: 234 100 100; www.hotel-yasmin.cz; €€€; metro: Muzeum; map p.134 C4

Just one block away from Wenceslas Square, this newly opened hotel has a more playful approach than some of the more po-faced designer hotels elsewhere in the city. Graced by loud contemporary artworks and with comfortable rooms (check out the sumptuous bathrooms), this is a winner. The chic noodle bar is not a bad place to eat either.

Pension Museum
Mezibranská 15; tel: 296 325 186; www.pension-museum.cz; €–€€; metro: Muzeum; map p.136 C1

This pension is in a convenient location just off Wenceslas Square. Well kept with a pleasant garden, the rooms are modern and clean with wooden floors. The large and airy accommodation is ideal for people with families, and the reasonable price includes a hearty buffet breakfast.

Penzion u šuterů
Palackého 4; tel: 224 948 235; www.usuteru.cz; €; metro: Muzeum; map p.134 B4

Great-value, if simple, rooms very close to Wenceslas Square. Part of the building dates back to 1383, and the Gothic vaulting can still be seen in the cellar. Now with a Baroque façade, the hotel is in a great location and has a decent restaurant attached.

Penzion u svatého Jana
Vyšehradská 28; tel: 224 911 789; www.usvjana.cz; €; metro: Karlovo Náměstí; map p.136 B3

Right next door to the Church

Drums' can be found opposite Kafka's House, in the Old Town. In this small, newly converted residence, you can choose between a room with an original painted wooden ceiling, one where the attached bathroom has a glass roof, or the two-storey attic apartment.

Nové Město

987 Prague
Senovázné náměstí 15; tel: 255 737 200; www.987hotels.com; €€€€; metro: Náměstí Republiky; map p.135 C3

In the north of the New Town is this über chic design hotel. Newly opened with Philippe Starck fixtures and Aera Saarinena and Arne Jacobsen furniture, it epitomises a certain kind of Northern European cool design. Great if you like it, but this is not the cheapest place in town. They are due to open a more funky take on the same theme, the 987 Soho, at Na Porící 42 during 2009.

Carlo IV
Senovázné náměstí 13; tel: 224 593 111; www.boscolo hotels.it; €€€€; metro: Náměstí Republiky; map p.135 C3

A very grand 19th-century building painstakingly converted into a luxury hotel. The interior designers have let their imaginations run riot with sumptuous rooms, a

---

chic restaurant and a fabulous spa and swimming pool. It can also be fabulously expensive, but perhaps worth it for this very Continental version of stylish comfort.

Hotel Elite
Ostrovní 32; tel: 224 932 250; www.hotelelite.cz; €; metro: Národní Trida; map p.134 B4

Not many hotels in the New Town have a suite protected by the municipality, but the Elite has, due to a 17th-century painted ceiling. The other rooms have also been tastefully preserved, with wooden floors, period furniture and an uncluttered feel. There is a pleasant courtyard bar and café for the summer, and the Ultramarin restaurant.

Hotel Palace
Panská 12; tel: 224 093 111; www.palacehotel.cz; €€€; metro: Mústek; map p.134 C3–4

A Secessionist landmark, built in 1909 as a luxury hotel. It still performs this function today, though now it is only the façade that retains its Art Nouveau appearance. The interior was gutted in the 1980s to

---

Price for a double room for one night without breakfast:
€ under €120
€€ €120–€180
€€€ €180–€250
€€€€ over €250

Right: view from Hotel Praha.

of St John on the Rock, this newish hotel is set in the church's neo-Baroque administrative annexe. The large rooms are fairly bare but clean, and the building is grand and in a quiet location.

Vyšherad
Pension Vyšehrad
Krokova 6, Vyšehrad; tel: 241 408 455; www.pension-vysehrad.cz; metro: Vyšehrad; €; map p.136 B4

A quiet, friendly, family-run pension with impressive views and a very attractive garden. There are only four simple but comfortable rooms, and a small dining room with a patio.

Smíchov and the Southwest
Andel's
Stroupežnického 21, Smíchov; tel: 296 889 688; www.andels hotel.com; €–€€; metro: Andél

Although this glass-and-steel hotel may seem a little corporate at first, it has nice designer touches, elegant rooms and a luxurious feel. This all comes at a surprisingly good price (due as much as anything to the location, but it is still only 10 minutes away from the centre by metro).

Angelo
Radlická 1, Smíchov; tel: 234 801 111; www.angelohotel.

com; €–€€; metro: Andél

Cheapish, cheerful and colourful, this designer hotel is quite a good place to stay outside of the city centre. The rooms are nicely done and the bathrooms are great. the building is perhaps better-looking on the outside than from the rather corporate corridors, but for a business hotel it is pretty decent.

Riverside Hotel
Janáčkovo nábřeží 15, Smíchov; tel: 225 994 611; www.riversideprague.com; €€€; metro: Andél

Not bad for a bit of 19th-century Prague and comfort, the luxurious rooms in this hotel are not too expensive considering what you get. Although it is a little way out, you do get great views over the river.

Holešovice
Hotel Absolut
Jablonského 4; Holešovice; tel: 222 541 406; www.absoluthotel. cz; €–€€; metro: Holešovice

This modern, somewhat business-style, hotel is a good place to stay if you are looking for a bit of luxury at a reasonable price. The rooms are nicely done (as are the bathrooms), and the hotel's bar is not bad as these things go, with some good cocktails.

Břevnov
Hotel Adalbert
Břevnovský klášter, Markétská 1, Břevnov; tel: 220 406 170; www.hoteladalbert.cz; €–€€; tram: 22, 36

This hotel is in an excellent and beautifully quiet location inside the Břevnov Monastery; convenient for both the city centre (by tram) and airport (by bus). The 18th-century building is very attractive and the comfortable rooms are excellent value.

Hotel Praha
Sušická 20, Dejvice; tel: 224 343 305; www.htlpraha.cz; €€€€; tram: 2, 8, 36

Out towards the airport, this 1980s Stalinist undulating concrete ziggurat has managed to turn its previous incarnation as a place exclusively for apparatchiks to its advantage; there is a certain chic to its Modernist bulk, large rooms and built-in security measures. Aside from these, there are garden terraces and excellent service.

Pension Pat'anka
Pat'anka 4, Dejvice; tel: 224 314 309; www.patanka.cz; €; metro: Dejvická

A bit out of the way, near the Hotel International, but quiet and well run, this pension has simple, comfortable rooms with en suite bathrooms. The prices are very reasonable and include breakfast.

Vinohrady and Žižkov
Pension 15
Vlkova 15, Žižkov; tel: 222 719 768; www.pension15.cz; €; tram: 5, 9, 26; map p.135 E4

Spotless if slightly spartan rooms with shared bathrooms and apartments at very good prices. Well run and modern, this is an excellent budget option not far from the tram stops on Seifertova. Cash only.

Jewish Prague

Prague's first Jewish community was founded in 1091. Despite oppression and laws restricting Jewish residents to a small area of the city, it flourished, becoming a focal point for Jewish culture in Central Europe. Religious freedom finally came with the Age of Enlightenment and Emperor Josef II's Patent of Toleration of 1781. The ghetto was later renamed Josefov in his honour. In 1848 the old segregation laws were at last repealed, although less than a century passed before the Nazis brought mass deportations, wiping out 90 percent of the population. Today, Prague's Jewish community numbers around 7,000.

The Jewish Museum

Office: U Staré školy 1; tel: 221 711 511; www.jewishmuseum. cz; sites: Sun–Fri winter 9am–4.30pm, summer 9am–6pm; admission charge; tram: 17, 53, metro: Staroměstská

In the 1890s, almost all of the Jewish Quarter (Josefov) was demolished. Everything was swept away except the Jewish Town Hall, several synagogues and the old cemetery. Today, most of these places –

According to legend, Rabbi Löw created a **'Golem'** to defend the Jewish Quarter after the emperor decreed that Prague's Jews were to be expelled or killed. The Rabbi made the golem using clay from the banks of the Vltava, and brought it to life with mystical Hebrew incantations. As the Golem grew, it became more violent and started killing gentiles. When the emperor rescinded his decree the Rabbi destroyed the Golem. Rabbi Löw stored the monster's remains in a coffin in the attic of the Old-New Synagogue so that it could be summoned again if needed.

with the notable exception of the Old-New Synagogue – form the city's Jewish Museum. A single ticket gains entrance to six sites.

Maisel Synagogue

Maiselova 10; map p.134 B2

Founded in the 1590s by Mordecai Maisel, the wealthy mayor of the quarter, it was destroyed in 1689 when a fire gutted much of the district. The present building was given its neo-Gothic appearance at the end of the 19th century. Inside is an exhibition of manuscripts, prints, textiles and liturgical silverware.

Pinkas Synagogue

Široká 3; map p.134 A2

Rabbi Pinkas founded this synagogue in 1479 after he had fallen out with the elders of the Old-New Synagogue. The present building came into being in 1535. Since 1958 the synagogue has served as a memorial to 77,297 of the Czech Jewish victims of the Holocaust.

The synagogue also serves as a memorial to the 7,500 children who died in Nazi concentration camps, and to the women who encouraged

them to paint and draw while they were awaiting deportation from the holding camp at Terezín, about 60km (38 miles) north of Prague.

Old Jewish Cemetery

Starý židovský hřbitov; entrance from Široká; map p.134 A2

The Old Jewish Cemetery came into being in the 15th century, and burials continued here until 1787. The number of graves is much greater than the 12,000 gravestones would suggest – the true figure is probably closer to 100,000. Because this was the only place where Jews could be buried, graves were piled layer on layer.

The oldest monument in the cemetery is the tombstone of the poet Avigdor Kara, dating from 1439. Also buried here, in 1601, was the noted Jewish mayor Mordecai Maisel. But the most famous tomb is that of the great scholar Rabbi Löw (1525–1609), who supposedly created the Golem *(see box, left).*

Ceremonial Hall

U starého hřbitova 3; map p.134 A2

Left: a roadside stall in Josefov.

only Jewish cemetery in Prague where funerals are still held. Many of the 25,000 graves are neglected and now covered in ivy. Most visitors come to the cemetery to see Franz Kafka's grave. To find it, follow the signpost from the main avenue east, turn right at row 21, and then when you reach the wall, turn left and walk to the end of that section.

Old-New Synagogue

Červená 2; tel: 224 819 456; www.synagogue.cz; Apr–Oct Sun–Thur 9.30am–5pm, Fri until 4pm; admission charge; tram: 17, 53, metro: Staroměstská; map p.134 A2

The synagogue dates back to the 1270s, and is the oldest Jewish house of worship still in use in Europe. The building is an unparalleled example of a medieval two-aisled synagogue, and the interior is remarkably original. It had been left unaltered as a tribute to the 3,000 people who sought sanctuary here yet were slaughtered in the pogrom of 1389. In the middle of the east wall is the Torah shrine, called the Ark. Next to the Ark is the Chief Rabbi's Chair. Among the other seats lining the walls is a tall one marked with a gold star. It belonged to Rabbi Löw.

Opposite the Old-New Synagogue on Červená is the **High Synagogue**, built into the **Old Town Hall**. Neither are open to the public for viewing. The town hall was designed in 1586 in Renaissance style. In keeping with the Hebrew practice of reading from right to left, the hands on the clock tower move in an anticlockwise direction.

The life of **Franz Kafka** (1883–1924), author of *The Trial* and other famous books, is inextricably linked with Prague's Jewish Quarter, having lived, worked and died here. For more about Kafka, *see Literature and Theatre, p.74*.

This neo-Romanesque building was built in 1911 for the Prague Burial Society. Inside is an exhibition devoted to Jewish life and traditions, with particular emphasis on medicine, illness and death.

Klausen Synagogue

U Starého hřbitova 1; map p.134 A2

This barrel-vaulted Baroque hall was built in 1694. It now houses an exhibition of Hebrew manuscripts, textiles and silverware.

Spanish Synagogue

Vězeňská 1; map p.134 B2

This restored Reform synagogue was built in 1868. The synagogue takes its name from the Moorish-style stucco decoration of the interior. On the ground floor is an exhibition on Jewish life in the region from the 19th century onwards. The first floor holds a collection of synagogue silver from Bohemia and Moravia.

Jerusalem Synagogue

Jeruzalémská 7; tel: 222 319 002; Apr–Oct Sun–Fri 1–5pm; admission charge; tram: 9, 14, 24, 51, 55, 58, metro: Hlavní Nádraží; map p.135 C3

The decision to build this synagogue was made in 1898, 50 years after the accession to the Austrian Throne of Franz Joseph I, who repealed the Jewish segregation laws in 1848. Consequently, it is also known as the Jubilee Synagogue. The building was designed by Viennese architect Wilhelm Stiassny in Art Nouveau style, drawing on Maori decorative idioms.

New Jewish Cemetery

Izraelská 1; tel: 226 235 248; www.kehilaprag.cz; Apr–Sept Sun–Thur 9am–5pm, Fri 9am–2pm, Oct–Mar Sun–Thur 9am–4pm, Fri 9am–2pm; free; metro: Želivského

Situated in Žižkov and founded in 1890, this is the

Language

For native English-speakers Czech appears to have an impenetrable vocabulary, a formidable array of accents and a complex grammar involving bewildering changes in the ending of words. Local people will not expect you to have mastered their language, but as in every country, they will be pleased if you have made the effort to acquire a few basics. One plus point is that Czech, unlike English, is pronounced exactly as it looks. A few – very few – words in international use can be deciphered; examples include *tramvaj* (tramway or tram), *recepce* (hotel reception) and *auto* (car).

Pronunciation

The stress in a word is always on the first syllable.

Vowels

Long vowels are indicated by an accent: á, é, í, ó, ú or ů and ý.
Ě like 'ye' in 'yes'
Ý long 'e' as in 'feet'
Au like 'ow' in 'now'
Ou like 'ow' in 'show'
L and r can be pronounced as half-vowels as in *Plzeň* (almost like Pulzen) = Pilsen, *krk* (almost like kirk) = neck.

Consonants

C ts as in 'its'
Č like 'ch' in 'church'
Ch like 'ch' in 'loch'
J like 'y' in yes
R trilled or rolled
Ř (unique to Czech, and even difficult for some natives) a combination of a trilled r and sh, as in Dvořák
Š 'sh'
Ž like 's' in pleasure

Basic Communication

Good morning/how do you do? Dobrý den
Good evening Dobrý večer
Good night Dobrou noc

Many people in the tourism industry know at least some English (and German), but you should not assume this; it is always polite to ask: *'Promiňte, mluvite anglicky?'* (Excuse me, do you speak English?)

Hello Ahoj
Goodbye Na shledanou
Yes Ano
No Ne
Please/you're welcome Prosím
Thank you Děkuji
Excuse me Promiňte
I'm sorry Je mi líto
How are you? Jak se máte? (This may be interpreted literally)
Fine, thanks Děkuji, dobře
And you? A vy?
Cheers! (when drinking) Na zdraví!
Help! Pomoc!
I am looking for... Hledám...
What? Co?
Where? Kde?
Where is/are? Kde je/jsou?
When? Kdy?
How? Jak?
How much? Kolik?

How much does it cost? Kolik to stojí?
I want Chci
We want Chceme
I would like Chtěl bych (chtěla bych if the speaker is female)
I don't know Nevím
I don't understand Nerozumím
Slowly, please! Pomalu, prosím!
Here Tady
There Tam

Numbers

0 Nula
1 Jeden, jedna (feminine), jedno (neuter)
2 Dva, dvě (feminine, neuter)
3 Tři
4 Čtyři
5 Pět
6 Šest
7 Sedm
8 Osm
9 Devět
10 Deset
11 Jedenáct
12 Dvanáct
13 Třináct
14 Čtrnáct
15 Patnáct
16 Šestnáct
17 Sedmnáct

Left: navigating Czech is less difficult than you'd expect.

What is the time? *Kolik je hodin?*
One o'clock *Jedna hodina*
Two/three/four o'clock *Dvě/tři/čtyři hodiny*
Five o'clock *Pět hodin*

Signs

Autobusové nádraží Bus station
Celnice Customs
Informace Information
Muži, páni Gentlemen
Nádraží Railway station (*Hlavní nádraží* main station)
Nástupiště Platform
Občerstvení Refreshments
Obsazeno Occupied, engaged
Odjezd/odchod Departure
Otevřeno Open
Pokladna Cash desk, booking office
Pozor Danger
Příjezd/příchod Arrival
Sem Pull
Směnárna Bureau de change
Tam Push
Vstup/vchod Entrance
Výstup/východ Exit
Záchod Lavatory (or WC, pronounced 'vay-tsay')
Zakázáno Forbidden (*Kouření zakázáno* No smoking)
Zastávka Tram/bus stop
Zavřeno Closed
Ženy, dámy Women, Ladies

18 *Osmnáct*
19 *Devatenáct*
20 *Dvacet*
21 *Dvacet jeden* (or *jednadvacet*)
22 *Dvacet dva* (or *dvaadvacet*)
30 *Třicet*
40 *Čtyřicet*
50 *Padesát*
60 *Šedesát*
70 *Sedmdesát*
80 *Osmdesát*
90 *Devadesát*
100 *Sto*
200 *Dvě stě*
300 *Tři sta*
400 *Čtyři sta*
500 *Pět set*
600 *Šest set*
1,000 *Tisíc*
1,000,000 *Milión*
A pair/few *Pár*
Half *Půl*

Times and Dates

Monday *pondělí*
Tuesday *úterý*
Wednesday *středa*
Thursday *čvrtek*
Friday *pátek*
Saturday *sobota*
Sunday *neděle*
January *leden*
February *únor*

March *březen*
April *duben*
May *květen*
June *červen*
July *červenec*
August *srpen*
September *září*
October *říjen*
November *listopad*
December *prosinec*
Day *Den*
Morning *Ráno*
Afternoon *Odpoledne*
Evening *Večer*
Night *Noc*
Yesterday *Včera*
Today *Dnes*
Tomorrow *Zítra*
Now *Teď*

TURISTICKÉ INFORMACE

Literature and Theatre

Prague has a rich literary heritage, providing the setting for the allegorical nightmares of Franz Kafka, the magic realism of Milan Kundera and the theatre of the absurd of its playwright-president, Václav Havel. Monuments to Kafka can be found in Josefov, to Neruda in Malá Strana, and to Hašek in Žižkov, while their legacy is preserved in the city's many bookshops and theatres. Prague also has a fine tradition of puppet theatre *(see Children, p.41)*, as well as a unique sideline in 'Black Light' mime shows, detailed below.

Franz Kafka

Franz Kafka (1883–1924) is probably the Czech Republic's most famous author (even though he wrote in German). His most famous works include *The Trial* (1925) and *The Castle* (1926), and concern troubled individuals in a nightmarishly impersonal and bureaucratic world. All his stories except *Metamorphosis* (1915) were published only after his early death from tuberculosis.

Franz Kafka Exhibition

U Radnice 5; tel: 224 227 452; Tue–Fri 10am–6pm, Sat 10am–5pm; admission charge; tram: 17, 53, metro: Staroměstská; map p.134 B3

Kafka was born in this building. Little remains of the original fabric – only the stone portal – after a fire in 1887. Inside you can see photographs and manuscript material relating to the writer.

Franz Kafka Museum

Cihelná 2; tel: 257 535 507; www.kafkamuseum.cz; daily 10am–6pm; admission charge; tram: 12, 18, 20, 22, 23, 57, metro: Malostranská; map p.133 D2

Situated on the other side of the river from Josefov, in Malá Strana, this exhibition charts Kafka's life with letters, photographs, first editions and audiovisual pieces.

Further Reading

LITERATURE

Chatwin, Bruce *Utz* (1988) Story of an obsessive porcelain collector living in Prague's Josefov.

Hašek, Jaroslav *The Good Soldier Švejk and His Fortunes in the World War* (1923) Anti-war novel following the adventures of the original Czech anti-hero.

Hrabal, Bohumil *I Served the King of England* (1971)

Left: bust of Kafka at the Kafka Museum.

Surreal experiences of another Prague anti-hero, a waiter who worked in the famous Hotel Paříž, then served, not the King of England, but his country's German occupiers.

Kundera, Milan *The Joke* (1967) Satire of life in Czechoslovakia under the communist regime.

There are numerous sights around Prague associated with Kafka. As a child, Kafka lived at U Mínuty House at no. 2 in the Old Town Square. He attended school at no. 12 (the Kinský Palace), where, in the same building, his father also had his haberdashery shop (now occupied by the Franz Kafka Bookstore). Later, at no. 5 (Oppelt House) he wrote most of The Castle, and then at no. 18, The House of the Unicorn, he frequented a literary salon. For worship, Kafka attended the Old-New Synagogue where his bar mitzvah was held.

Left and below: Kafka is Prague's most famous son of a renown literary scene.

Bookshops

Anagram Bookshop
Týn 4; tel: 224 895 737; www.anagram.cz; Mon–Sat 10am–8pm, Sun 10am–7pm; tram: 5, 8, 14, metro: Náměstí Republiky; map p.134 B3
Characterful bookshop within the Týn courtyard, selling books on Prague, an array of other subjects and even some second-hand books in English.

Big Ben
Malá Štupartská 5; tel: 224 826 565; www.bigbenbook shop.com; Mon–Fri 9am–6.30pm, Sat–Sun 10am–5pm; tram: 5, 8, 14, metro: Náměstí Republiky; map p.134 B3
English-language bookshop, selling fiction, travel guides, children's books, selected non-fiction, newspapers and magazines.

Globe Bookstore and Coffeehouse
Pštrossova 6; tel: 224 934 203; www.globebookstore.cz; daily 9.30am–midnight; tram: 17, 21; map p.136 A1
An ex-pat institution, this store stocks books, newspapers and magazines in a variety of languages, as well as housing a pleasant café.

SEE ALSO CAFÉS AND BARS, P.32

Meyrink, Gustav *The Golem* (1913)
Classic retelling of the legend of Rabbi Löw's monster moulded from clay.
Neruda, Jan *Prague Tales* (1877)
Also known as *Tales of Malá Strana* (Lesser Quarter).
Rilke, Rainer Maria *Two Stories of Prague* (1899)
Stories about the German community in Prague by one of its own sons.

HISTORY AND BIOGRAPHY

Brod, Max *Franz Kafka: a Biography* (1937)
Biography by Kafka's friend, editor and literary executor.
Demetz, Peter *Prague in Black and Gold: the History of a City* (1997)
Thematic account by an exile who is now a professor at Yale.
Garton Ash, Timothy *We the People* (1990)
Eyewitness account of the events of 1989 by a British journalist and academic.
Havel, Václav *To the Castle and Back* (2007)

Political memoir by the playwright and former president.
Ripellino, Angelo Maria *Magic Prague* (1993)
Eccentric literary and cultural history of Prague.

Right: Globe Bookstore.

For listings of what's on at the theatre, consult the Culture in Prague website at www.ceskakultura.cz/praha-divadla, visit the website of the Prague Information Service at www.pis.cz, or pick up a copy of *Prague Post* (www.praguepost.cz) for details of fringe theatre.

Judaica

Široká 7; Mon–Fri 10am–6pm, Sun 10am–4pm; tram: 17, 53, metro: Staroměstská; map p.134 A2

Shop specialising in Jewish books and prints, both second-hand and new.

Kavárna Řehoř Samsa
Vodičkova 30 (pasáž U Nováků); tel: 224 225 413; 9.30am–7pm; tram: 3, 9, 14, 24, 52, 53, metro: Můsek; map p.134 B4

Excellent bookshop-cum-café tucked away in one of the passages off the Lucerna shopping arcade.
SEE ALSO CAFÉS AND BARS, P.33

Makovský-Gregor
Kaprova 9; tel: 223 283 35; Mon–Fri 9am–7pm, Sat–Sun 10am–6pm; tram: 17, 53, metro:

Staroměstská; map p.133 E2

Old-fashioned second-hand book dealer, with a stock that includes a selection of English books.

Shakespeare and Sons
Krymská 12; tel: 271 740 839; daily 10am–7pm; www.shakes.cz; metro: Staroměstská; map p.137 E3

Excellent English-language bookseller, with a second branch at U Luzickeho seminare 10 in Malá Strana (tel: 257 531 894).

Theatre

Estates Theatre (Stavorské divadlo)
Ovocný trh 1; tel: 224 215 001; www.estatestheatre.cz; box office open daily 10am–6pm; tram: 3, 9, 14, 24, metro: Můstek; map p.134 B3

The neoclassical Estates Theatre originally opened in 1783 as the Nostitz Theatre, named after Count Nostitz who paid for it. In its earlier history, it played largely to upper-class German audiences, hence its current name – the 'Estates' were the German nobility. Famously,

Right: Estates Theatre.

this was where Mozart conducted the premiere of *Don Giovanni* in 1787. Nowadays, the theatre is a second home for the National Theatre company, presenting a programme of high-quality theatre, opera, ballet and dance. Tours of the theatre are available daily (tel: 224 902 231).

National Theatre
Národní třída 2; tel: 224 901 448; www.narodni-divadlo.cz; box office open daily 10am–6pm; tram: 6, 9, 17, 18, 22, 23, metro: Národní Třída; map p.134 A4

The National Theatre and its magnificent building were the product of the Czech 'national awakening' in the later 19th century. Today, the company stages productions of drama, opera and ballet at this location as well as at the Estates Theatre *(see left)*. They also have the use of the Kolowrat Theatre – across the road from the Estates Theatre at Ovocný trh 6 – for 'chamber plays' and rehearsals. Tours

of the theatre on Národní třída are available daily (tel: 224 901 506).

Palác Akropolis
Kubelíkova 27; tel: 296 330 911; www.palacakropolis.cz; daily 11am–1am; metro: Jiřího z Poděbrad; map p.135 E4

The theatre in this Art Deco arts complex in Žižkov presents a programme of modern theatre and dance as well as musical theatre.
SEE ALSO NIGHTLIFE, P.104

Black Light Theatre
Black Light Theatre, or Černé divadlo, first became popular in Prague in late 1950s. Its effect is created by actors rendered invisible by being dressed all in black, fluorescent paints and clever lighting techniques. Most performances are mimes involving an element of dance and pantomime. Nowadays, productions are aimed at tourists and are rarely artistically distinguished.

Black Light Theatre of Jiří Srnec
Národní 20; tel: 257 923 397; box office open daily 9am–7.30pm; tram: 6, 9, 17, 18, 22, 23, metro: Národní Třída; map p.134 A4

Probably the best of the Black Light Theatre companies, staging productions without the worst of the usual sentimentality and kitsch.

Image Theatre
Pařížská 4; tel: 222 314 448; www.imagetheatre.cz; box office open daily 9am–8pm; tram: 17, 18, metro: Staroměstská; map p.134 B2

The emphasis here is on dance and modern jazz, presenting a modern take on the Black Light genre.

Magic Lantern
Národní třída 4; tel: 224 931 482; www.laterna.cz; box office open Mon–Sat 10am–8pm; tram: 6, 9, 17, 18, 22, 23, metro: Národní Třída; map p.134 B4

Next door to the National Theatre is the Nová Scéna, a controversial modern glass construction, built to designs by Karel Prager in 1983. The productions are more high-tech than the competition, though the material is not as imaginative as it might be.

Left: the National Theatre.

Monuments

Prague has had such an eventful history that it is unsurprising that there are so many monuments bearing testimony to great events. This chapter lists alphabetically the most important memorials to religious strife, political ambition, civic pride and even celebrity culture. Other monuments of importance can be found elsewhere in this book. See *Architecture (p.26–9), Castles, Palaces and Houses (p.34–9) and Jewish Prague (p.70–71)*. The chapter on *History (see p.62–3)* may also be helpful in familiarising yourself with the kings, wars and sequence of events to which many of the monuments relate.

Charles Bridge

Křižovnické náměstí to Mostecká; tram: 17, 18, 53, metro: Staroměstská; map p.134 A3

The Charles Bridge was commissioned by Charles IV in 1357 to replace the earlier Judith Bridge, which collapsed in a flood in 1342. Completed in about 1400, it was built by Petr Parléř, who also designed St Vitus's Cathedral *(see p.44)*.

On the Staré Město (Old Town) side is Parléř's **Old Town Bridge Tower** (tel: 224 220 569; daily May–Oct 10am–10pm, winter closing times vary

Right: Charles Bridge statue.

between 5pm and 7pm; admission charge). It was here that in 1648, at the end of the Thirty Years War, an army of Swedish invaders was fought off by a band of Prague townspeople. Despite being damaged in the fracas, much of the sculptural decoration has survived. Look on the external corners for the figures of 14th-century gropers feeling up buxom ladies.

The tower contains an exhibition on the history of the building since its construction commenced in 1373.

Crossing the bridge itself, you pass a succession of statues and monuments, most of which are copies of the Baroque originals. The earliest of these is a crucifix (third on the right) erected in 1657. In 1696, a Jewish man was found guilty of blaspheming in front of the crucifix and was made to pay for the gold Hebrew inscription that reads, 'Holy, Holy, Holy Lord God Almighty'.

The most famous statue on the bridge is that of St John of Nepomuk (eighth on the right), placed here in 1683. King Wenceslas IV was supposed to have had this priest killed after he refused to divulge the contents of the queen's confession; he was dressed up in a suit of armour and thrown over the side of the bridge.

At the Malá Strana (Lesser Town) end are two towers. The shorter one was originally part of the 12th-century Judith Bridge that preceded the Charles Bridge. The taller

Right: Hus Memorial.

Jan Žižka – after whom the district of Žižkov was named in 1877 – was a military commander who had fought for the English at the battle of Agincourt in 1415. After the Hussite uprising on 30 July 1419, he was chosen as leader of the Reformationist forces.

He conquered Emperor Sigismund's army, captured Prague at the battle of Vítkov Hill (present-day Žižkov) in 1421 and, famously, lost both eyes in battle.

Left: relief from the Charles Bridge.

fall of the Habsburg Empire to the invasion of the Warsaw Pact troops in 1968.

John Lennon Wall

Velkopřevorské náměstí; tram: 12, 20, 22, 23, 57; map p.133 D2

This graffiti-strewn shrine to John Lennon, on the garden wall of the Palace of the Grand Prior of the Knights of Malta, faces onto a pretty square in Malá Strana. During the 1980s, it was the focus of Prague's Beatles-worship. The 'mural' was twice under threat: first from the secret police, who painted over it, and then from the Knights of Malta, who objected to the graffiti once the property had been returned to them under the post-1989 restitution. The wall was finally saved from respectability by the intervention of the French ambassador, who lived opposite and who appealed to the authorities to let it be.

National Monument

U památníku 1900; tel: 222 781 676; metro: Florenc

The National Memorial on Žižkov Hill was originally

one (on the right) is the **Malá Strana Bridge Tower** (tel: 242 441 586; daily mid-Mar–Oct 10am–6pm; admission charge) and was built from 1464 in imitation of the tower on the Staré Město side of the bridge. Inside is an exhibition on the history of the bridge, though it is the views from the top that justify the entrance fee.

Hus Memorial

Staroměstské náměstí; tram: 17, 18, 53, metro: Staroměstská; map p.134 B3

This imposing memorial in the middle the Old Town Square honours the great Protestant reformer Jan Hus. It was erected on the 500th anniversary – 6 July 1915 – of his being burnt at the stake. The work of Czech sculptor Ladislav Šaloun, it features Hussites and Protestants around the figure of Hus, together with a mother and child symbolising rebirth. Since its unveiling, it has formed a symbol of resistance to foreign occupation, from the

Left: the Rozhledna Observation Tower.

Observation Tower

Rozhledna; tel: 257 320 112; daily Apr and Sept 10am–7pm, May–Aug 10am–10pm, Oct 10am–6pm, Nov–Mar Sat–Sun 10am–5pm; admission charge; tram: 12, 20, 22, 23, 57 then funicular; map p.132 B3

At the top of Petřín Hill is a replica of the Eiffel Tower, standing at a height of 60m (197ft) – only a fifth of the height of the original – but offering spectacular views of the city (and in good weather, even to the forests of Central Bohemia). It was constructed out of old railway tracks in 31 days for Prague's 1891 Jubilee Exhibition. During the Nazi occupation, however, Hitler wanted to have it removed because he felt it ruined the view from his room in the castle.

SEE ALSO PARKS AND GARDENS, P.108

Old Town Hall

Staroměstské náměstí 1; tel: 724 508 584; Mar–Oct Tue–Sun 9am–6pm, Mon 11am–6pm, Nov–Feb Tue–Sun 9am–5pm, Mon 11am–5pm; admission charge; tram: 17, 18, 53, metro: Straroměstská; map p.134 B3

built in 1929–30, though was remodeled under the communists as a Tomb of the Unknown Soldier and as a mausoleum for communist leaders. As part of the reconstruction, a splendid series of bronze reliefs were added, depicting valiant revolutionaries and heroic workers. In front of the memorial is a massive equestrian statue of General Žižka *(see box, p.78)*. At the time of writing, the monument was undergoing extensive renovation and was closed to the public.

Founded in 1338, the Old Town Hall was composed from a collection of medieval buildings, purchased one by one over the years with the proceeds of the city's tax on wine. It is most famous today for the **Astronomical Clock** on its side.

This mechanical wonder dates originally from 1410 – although it was transformed into the contraption you see today by one Master Hanuš in 1490. According to legend he was blinded after completing his work so that he could not replicate it anywhere else. He got his revenge by climbing into the mechanism and disabling it. Documentary evidence suggests, however, that he continued to maintain the clock, unblinded, for many years, though the clock did not work properly until it was overhauled in 1570.

The performance of the upper part of the clock draws hordes of tourists at the striking of the hour from 8am to 8pm. Death rings the death knell and turns an hourglass upside down. The 12 Apostles proceed along the little windows which open before the chimes, and a cockerel flaps its wings and crows.

While famous elsewhere as the 'Good King Wenceslas' of the Christmas carol, to the Czechs **Wenceslas** was not a king at all, but the Duke of Bohemia and their country's patron saint. He lived c.907–35 and was brought up as a Christian by his grandmother, St Ludmila, before taking the reins of state, founding the church of St Vitus's (now the cathedral) and then being murdered on the orders of his younger brother while on his way to church. His feast day is 28 September, and since the year 2000 this day has been celebrated as a national holiday.

The hour strikes. To the right of Death, a Turk wags his head. The two figures on the left are allegories of Greed and Vanity.

The face of the clock underneath preserves the medieval view of the course of the sun and moon through the zodiac, with Prague and the earth located at the centre of the universe. Beneath that is the calendar, with signs of the zodiac and scenes from country life, symbolising the 12 months of the year. The calendar is a replica of the work executed by Czech painter Josef Mánes in 1866 and now in the Prague City Museum (see p.91).

Just near the clock is the main entrance to the Town Hall itself. Tours take in the 15th-century council chamber, Petr Parléř's Gothic chapel (with a view of the interior workings of the clock), as well as the dungeons, which were used by the Czech resistance as their HQ during the Prague uprising at the end of World War II. Separate tickets can be purchased for access to the stairs or lift up the tower.

Statue of St Wenceslas

Václavské náměstí; tram: 11, metro: Muzeum; map p.136 C1
In a commanding position, at the southern end of Wenceslas Square in front of the National Museum, is the equestrian statue of St Wenceslas. It was erected in 1912, after 30 years of planning and design by Josef Myslbek. The base, designed by Alois Dryák, depicts SS Agnes, Adelbert, Procopius and Ludmila (Wenceslas's grandmother). It was from here that Alois Jirásek read the proclamation of Czechoslovakian independence to the assembled crowds on 28 October 1918.

Television Tower

Mahlerovy sady 1; tel: 242 418 778; www.tower.cz; daily 10am–11pm; admission charge; tram: 5, 9, 11, 26, 55, metro: Jiřího z Poděbrad; map p.135 E4
Located in Mahler Park, the TV Tower, at 216m (708ft), is the boldest architectural creation in Prague from the communist era. Inspired by the similar tower on Alexanderplatz in Berlin, it was designed by Václav Aulický and Jiří Kozák, and built between 1985 and 1991. Even before it was finished, it was supposed to have been used for blocking foreign broadcasts from the West.

Nowadays, you can take the lift up to the viewing platform at 93m (305ft). The cube-like rooms suspended on the towers each have an annotated map pointing out what you can see. Below the viewing platform is a restaurant offering spectacular views.

Left: the face of the Astronomical Clock. **Right:** the Television Tower.

Museums and Galleries

Prague is rich in museums and galleries, with displays on fine art, history and technology. Many visitors will not want to miss the collections of the National Gallery, particularly its holdings of modern art; and the Dvořák, Smetana and Mozart museums will provide plenty to please music enthusiasts. Prague is also home to some eccentric institutions. Few will not be surprised by the extraordinary contents of the Police Museum, the Náprstek Ethnographic Museum or the Miniature Museum.

Malá Strana

Czech Museum of Music
(České muzeum hudby)
Karmelitská 2; tel: 257 257 777; www.nm.cz; Wed–Mon 10am–6pm; admission charge; tram: 12, 20, 22, 23; map p.133 C2

The recently opened Czech Museum of Music is attractively housed in a converted Malá Strana church. As well as a wide variety of beautifully displayed instruments, there are enough interactive facilities guaranteed to make a visit entertaining as well as educational. The exhibits take you from popular music of the 20th century, via microtonal and folk instruments, to stringed instruments of the 17th century.

Kampa Gallery
U Sovových mlýnů 2; tel: 257 286 147; www.museum kampa.cz; daily 10am–6pm; admission charge; tram: 12, 20, 22, 23, 57; map p.133 D3

This converted watermill is situated on the banks of the Vltava in Kampa Park. It has several modern additions, including a staircase that leads up to a glass cube on top of the building, offering

Above: Kampa Gallery.

excellent views. There is also a glass footbridge, designed by Czech artist Václav Cigler, which appears to lead you out over the river. The proximity of the river ensured, of course, that the museum was inundated by the 2002 floods. The large sculpture of a chair standing on the embankment outside was washed 40km (25 miles) downstream.

Based around the collections of wealthy Czech expats Jan and Meda Mladek, the museum has large holdings of the works of the

abstract painter František Kupka (1871–1963) and the Expressionist and Cubist sculptor Otto Gutfreund (1889–1927). A good portion of the exhibition space is given over to displays of contemporary Central European art.

Komensky Pedagogical Museum
Valdštejnská 20; tel: 257 533 455; www.pmjak.cz; Tue–Sat 10am–12.30pm and 1–5pm; admission charge; tram: 12, 20, 22, 23, metro: Malostranská; map p.133 C1

This small museum charts the development of education, as based on the works of the Czech philosopher Comenius (1592–1670). The permanent exhibition features a reconstructed school room and glass cases displaying rare books and other documentary sources.

Hradčany

Kinský Villa
Kinského zahrada 97; tel: 257 214 806; www.nm.cz; May–Sept Tue–Sun 10am–6pm, Oct–Apr Tue–Sun 9am–5pm; admission charge; tram: 6, 9, 12, 20, metro:

Left: Dvorak Museum, *see p.90.*

small rooms. Mr Konyenko used to manufacture tools for eye microsurgery, but has since diverted his talents into inscribing a prayer on a human hair, creating images of cars on the leg of a mosquito, fashioning a pair of horseshoes for a flea and making the world's smallest book.

Prague Castle Picture Gallery (Obrazárna Pražského hradu)

Správa Pražského hradu; tel: 224 373 531; www.obrazarna-hradu.cz; daily Apr–Oct 9am–6pm, Nov–Mar 9am–4pm; admission charge; metro: Malostranská; map p.132 C1

The collection of the Prague Castle Picture Gallery was largely put together by art-lover Emperor Rudolf II (1583–1611). This emperor has gone down in history as something of an eccentric, yet he was a great patron of the arts and sciences and collected a huge amount of art treasures, as well as countless curiosities. His collection was one of the most notable in Europe in his day. When the imperial residence moved to Vienna, a great part of the collection went with it. Still more fell to the Swedes as loot during

---

The collections of **Prague's National Gallery** are spread out over several different sites: the Old Masters are in the Sternberg Palace; Baroque art is held opposite in the Schwarzenberg; art from the Middle Ages is on display in the Convent of St Agnes; 19th-century art is spread between St George's Convent and the Kinský Palace; the House of the Black Madonna is dedicated to Czech Cubism; 20th- and 21st-century art can be seen in the Trade Fair Palace; and, finally, the holdings of Asian art are in the Zbraslav Château just outside the city.

methods and handicrafts. There are regular folk concerts and demonstrations of crafts such as blacksmithing and woodcarving.

Miniature Museum

Strahovské nádvoří 11, tel: 233 352 371; www.muzeum miniatur.com; daily 9am–5pm; admission charge; tram: 22, 23; map p.132 B2

The Miniature Museum is located within the main courtyard of the Strahov Monastery. Here you can observe the handiwork of Siberian technician Anatoly Konyenko with the aid of microscopes arranged around the walls of two

---

Anděl; map p.132 C4

In the most southerly corner of the park on Petřín Hill is the Kinský family's former summer retreat, now the Musaion and a branch of the National Museum. It houses the ethnographic collection, with displays on traditional Czech folk culture and art, music, costume, farming

Right: the view of the Vltava from Kampa Gallery.

the Thirty Years War. Yet another valuable collection was created, during the 16th century, from what remained, but much of it was also taken to Vienna, or sold to Dresden. What was left was auctioned off, and was thought to be totally lost. After a long and tortuous history, the remnants of the Rudolfine collection, which decorated the castle apartments, were finally brought together and put on display in 1965. The gallery was closed from 1993–8 to reconstruct the space that you can now see.

The small but valuable collection contains almost 4,000 paintings (some of the most important are on permanent loan to the National Gallery), of which around 70 are on display at any one time. Among these are pieces by, among others: Hans von Aachen (*Head of a Girl*, 1611); Titian (*Young Woman at Her Toilet*, 1512–15); Tintoretto; Veronese; Rubens (*Assembly of the Gods at Olympos*, 1602); Matthias Bernard Braun; Adriaen de Vries; and the Bohemian Baroque artists Jan Kupecký and Petr Brandl.

Schwarzenberg Palace (Schwarzenberský palác)
Hradčanské náměstí 2; tel: 233 081 713; www.ngprague.cz; Tue–Sun 10am–6pm; admission charge; tram: 22, 23; map p.132 B2

Dominating Hradčanské náměstí is the sgraffito façade of the Renaissance Schwarzenberg Palace. This has been beautifully renovated and is now home to the National Gallery's collection of Baroque Art in Bohemia. There are three floors of galleries, starting with the paintings on the top two (avoid the transparent lift and landings if you get vertigo) and with sculpture on the ground floor.

Of the Mannerist pieces here, some of the most attractive are by Bartholomeus Spranger (*Resurrection*, 1576), Hans von Aachen (*Portrait of Painter Joseph Heintz*, 1585–7) and Roelant Savery (*Woodland Stream*, 1608). The first signs of Baroque painting in Bohemia are seen in the works of Karel Škréta (1610–74). Notable in the collection is his *Family Portrait of the Gem Carver Dionysio Miseroni* (*c.*1663).

There are also some fine works by the contemporaries Petr Brandl (1668–1735) and Jan Kupecký (1667–1740). Notable works are, by the former, *Bust of an Apostle* (*c.*1725), and by Kupecký, *Self-Portrait* (1711), which shows the artist working on a portrait of his wife. The Rococo is represented by a large collection of the works of Norbert Grund (1717–67); see his *Gallant Scene with a Lady on a Swing* (*c.*1760).

Sternberg Palace (Sternberský palác)
Hradčanské náměstí 15; tel: 220 514 634; www.ng prague.cz; Tue–Sun 10am–6pm; admission charge; tram: 22, 23; map p.132 B1

This houses the National Gallery's collection of European painting from the Classical Era to the end of the Baroque. While there is not the breadth of other national collections, the galleries contain some exceptionally fine works. The Sternberský palác is the town residence built in 1707 by Count Wenzel Adalbert Sternberg.

The gallery is set out on three levels: the ground floor houses German and Austrian

Left: Schwarzenberg Palace's collection of Baroque Art.

art from the 15th to the 18th century; the first floor comprises the art of antiquity, icons and the art of the Netherlands and Italy of the 14th–16th centuries; the second floor has Italian, Spanish, French, Dutch and Flemish art of the 16th–18th centuries. On the ground floor, opening onto the courtyard, is a pleasant café.

Albrecht Dürer's large-scale *Feast of the Rosary* (1506) is perhaps the most outstanding work in the gallery. One of the greatest paintings of the northern Renaissance, it combines the innovations of light and colour of Italian art, while retaining the northern Gothic tradition of the truthful portrayal of landscape and nature. Dürer himself can be seen on the right-hand side, holding a sheet of paper. Other wonderful pictures of the German and Austrian collection include the left and right wings of the *Hohenburg Altarpiece* (1509) by Hans Holbein the elder, and a number of paintings by Lucas Cranach the elder, including *St Christina* (c.1520–2) and *Adam and Eve* (c.1538).

Bronzino's wonderful portrait of *Eleonora of Toledo* (c.1540–3) is one of the many fine Italian paintings in the collection. Other works of interest include the *Portrait of an Elderly Man* (1580–90) by Bassano and *St Jerome* (c.1550) by Tintoretto.

Of large holdings of Flemish and Dutch paintings look out for Geertgen tot Sint

Jans's *Triptych with the Adoration of the Magi* (c.1490–95) and a panel by Jan Gossaert's (Mabuse) *St Luke Drawing the Virgin* (c.1513), which clearly shows the technique of perspective he learnt from Italian painters. Other Flemish and Dutch masterpieces include Rubens's painting *The Marchese Ambrogio Spinola* (c.1627), one of the finest portraits in the collection. Close by is another highlight, Rembrandt's *The Scholar in His Study* (1634), perhaps showing the 16th-century physician Paracelsus.

The *Still Life with a Goblet of Wine* by the German-Dutch painter Abraham Mignon (1640–79) is one of a number of exquisite still lifes in the gallery, including *Flowers in an Earthen Vase* by Jan Brueghel the elder (1568–1625).

Of the gallery's holdings of French and Spanish paintings, three in particular stand out: Simon Vouet's *Suicide of Lucretia* (c.1624–5); a painting by El Greco (Domenikos Theotokopoulos), *Christ in Prayer* (c.1595–7); and, finest of all, Goya's *Portrait*

Right: the Schwarzenberg Palace interior and distinctive ramparts.

The collection contains doll's houses, toy cars, motorbikes, aeroplanes and trains, toy farms, clockwork puppets, hundreds of Barbie dolls, tin robots and lots of teddy bears.

Staré Město

Charles Bridge Museum

Křížovnické náměstí 3; tel: 739 309 551; daily May–Oct 10am–8pm, Nov–Apr 10am–6pm; admission charge; tram: 17, 18, 53, metro: Staroměstská; map p.134 A3

This museum is located in a former monastic hospital, next door to the domed Church of St Francis at the Staré Město end of the Charles Bridge. As well as an exhibition on the history of the bridge, you can see the foundations of the earlier Judith Bridge which was swept away by floods in 1342. There is also access here to an underground chapel adapted from the vaults of an earlier Gothic church on the site. It is decorated in grotto-style, with stalactites made out of dust and eggshells.

of Don Miguel de Lardizabal (1815).

Strahov Collection of Art

Strahovské nádvoří 1; tel: 233 107 711; www.strahovsky klaster.cz; daily 9am–noon, 12.30–5pm; admission charge; tram: 22, 23; map p.132 A2

These newly renovated galleries can be found in the second courtyard of the Strahov precinct, accessed behind the monastery church. The works of art are mostly religious, though there are also secular works by Baroque and Rococo painters, including Norbert Grund (1717–67) and Franz Anton Maulbertsch (1724–96). One of the most important works on display is the wooden *Strahov Madonna*, by a mid-14th-century Czech sculptor. There is also a wonderful *Judith* from the workshop of Lucas Cranach the Elder (1472–1553).

Toy Museum

Jiřská 6; tel: 224 372 294; www.muzeumhracek.cz; daily 9.30am–5.30pm; admission charge; tram: 12, 18, 22, 23, metro: Malostranská; map p.133 C1

Located in the former Burgrave's house within Prague Castle, this museum displays the private toy collection of Ivan Steiger, a filmmaker and cartoonist.

Right: Kafka went to school at the Goltz Kinsky Palace.

Ethnographic Museum (Náprstkovo muzeum)

Betlémské náměstí 1; tel: 224 497 500; www.aconet.cz/npm; Tue–Sun 10am–6pm; admission charge; tram: 6, 9, 17, 18, 22, 23, metro: Národní Třída; map p.134 A3

This museum is named after Vojta Náprstek (1826–94). His fortune derived from brewing, and he chose to spend it on his two passions – ethnography and technology. His gadgets are now in the National Technical Museum *(see p.96)*, while his Asian, African and American collections are housed here, in the former brewery. He also established here the country's first women's club, and its meeting room has been preserved just as it was, complete with the hole Náprstek had drilled through the wall from his office.

The ground floor holds temporary exhibitions, while the first floor has the permanent collection of American Indian cultures. Among the exhibits are feathered Apache headdresses, some beautiful papooses from California and fine Inuit garments. The galleries continue with the Central and South American holdings, featuring brightly coloured textiles and stylised Huaxtec figures.

On the second floor are Australian, Polynesian and Melanesian exhibits: Aboriginal paintings, boomerangs and harpoons, and a lovely model of a fish. Look out

especially for the decorated skulls from the Solomon Islands and, of course, the large totem pole from Papua New Guinea. The museum's collection has also recently been augmented with private donations of two significant groups of African sculpture.

Goltz Kinsky Palace (Goltz-Kinský palác)

Staroměstské náměstí 12; tel: 224 810 758; www.ngprague.cz; Tue–Sun 10am–6pm; admission charge; tram: 17, 18, 53, metro: Straroměstská; map p.134 B3

In the northeast corner of the Old Town Square is the Rococo Goltz-Kinský palác, designed by Kilián Ignaz Dientzenhofer. It was from here in February 1948 that communist leader Klement Gottwald made the speech that heralded in the totalitar-

ian regime. The building now houses the National Gallery's collection of Czech landscape painting from the 17th to the 20th century. The ground-floor bookshop once formed the premises of Franz Kafka's father's haberdashery shop. Franz himself attended school elsewhere in the building.

House of the Black Madonna (Dům u Černé Matky Boží)

Ovocný trh 19; tel: 224 211 746; www.ngprague.cz; Tue–Sun 10am–6pm; admission charge; metro: Náměstí Republiky; map p.134 B3

The Cubist House of the Black Madonna was designed by Joseph Gočár (1911–12), originally as a department store. The second to fourth floors now contain the National Gallery's Museum of Czech Cubism.

The entrance is via a beautiful spiralling staircase with a Cubist motif on the bannister supports. The permanent galleries start on the second floor with a series of reliefs by Otto Gutfreund (look for *Při toaletě*, 1911). Also here is a wonderful display of ceramics by Pavel Janák (1882–1956), a number of Braque-like collage paintings by Emil Filla

Left: Strahov Monastery's collection. **Right:** Totem pole from the Ethnography Museum and the Black Madonna.

(1882–1953) and some excellent furniture by Gočár. The third floor contains a number of interesting architectural designs by Janák, as well as fine examples of his furniture. Further examples of Cubist design can be seen in the posters of Jaroslav Benda (1882–1970). The fourth floor is home to a striking series of prints by Bohumil Kubišta (1884–1918) and a collection of African statues from which he was said to have drawn his inspiration. However, the star exhibit is probably the building itself, as beautifully designed inside as out.

House of the Stone Bell
Staroměstské náměstí 13; tel: 224 827 526; www.citygallery prague.cz; Tue–Sun 10am–6pm; admission charge; tram: 17, 18, 53, metro: Straroměstská; map p.134 B3
This 14th-century Gothic building is one of the venues used by the Prague City Gallery to host temporary exhibitions of contemporary art. Other venues include the nearby House of the Golden Ring (Týnská 6; tel: 224 827 022) and the second

floor of the Old Town Hall (Staromůstské náměstí 1; tel: 224 482 751).

Museum of Decorative Arts (Umělecko-průmyslové muzeum)
17 listopadu 2; tel: 251 093 111; www.upm.cz; Tue–Sun 10am–6pm; admission charge; metro: Staroměstská; map p.134 A2
The building of the Museum of Decorative Arts is itself a fine example of Czech late 19th-century design, built 1897–1900. This is one of the best, and most interesting, museums in Prague. The beautifully arranged exhibits are displayed by process and material: 'The Story of Fibre' (textiles and fashion); 'Born in Fire' (ceramics and glass); 'Treasury' (metals); and 'Print & Image' (graphic design and photography).

Each section has some wonderful items, but among the best are the collections of late 19th- and 20th-century women's costume. Among many fine pieces are an adventurous day dress in a hand-woven fabric (1926) by Marie Teinitzerová, a 1930s sunbathing outfit of a bodice,

shorts and sleeveless jacket, and two great 1960s Op-Art-influenced swimsuits. The collections include not only clothing but an excellent selection of shoes and accessories.

The glass and ceramics collection includes some fine examples of 16th- to 17th-century Venetian glass, but, of course, it is the Bohemian work that is best represented. Of particular interest are the four cases that show the development of faience, glass and ceramics from Art Nouveau, via Cubism, Art Deco and the 1950s, to the present day.

Of the imaginatively displayed metalwork, it is probably those pieces of 1900–30 that are most interesting; look out for Josef Gočár's Cubist clock (1913). There are also some interesting examples of 20th-century jewellery, particularly those pieces from the 1970s and 1980s by Jozef Soukup.

The Czechs have long had a reputation for good graphic design, and this is borne out by the displays of

Left and below: Museum of Decorative Arts.

early 20th-century posters; chief among these are those displaying the influence of Cubism. As well as a display of experimental photography from the *fin de siècle* to the 1940s, there is a case of drawers showing the changes in typographical design from the 15th–20th centuries.

St Agnes's Convent (Anežský klášter)
U Milosrdných 17; tel: 224 810 628; www.ngprague.cz; Tue–Sun 10am–6pm; admission charge; metro: Staroměstská; map p.134 B2

St Agnes's Convent is the first early Gothic building in Prague (founded 1234). However, the whole complex, which included two convents and several churches, fell into decay over the years and parts of it were completely destroyed. After many years, restorers succeeded in bringing some rooms back to their original state. These were linked to form the present-day historic complex by means of carefully reconstructed additions.

The convent buildings now hold the National Gallery's collection of Medieval Art in Bohemia and Central Europe. The superb collection has been sensitively displayed and fits well into the restored space.

The exhibits are shown in broadly chronological order, starting with a very important early wooden statue, the *Madonna of Strakonice* (*c.*1300–20), and the painting of the *Madonna of Zbraslav* (1350–60). Among the star exhibits are the museum's two Bohemian altarpieces: the first from Vyšší Brod (1350), with a Nativity show-

The city's **Aircraft Museum** is on the outskirts of Prague at Kbely (Letecké muzeum, Mladoboleslavká 902; tel: 973 207 500; May–Oct Tue–Sun 10am–6pm; bus: 110, 259, 280 from Českomoravská metro, 185 from Palmovka metro). The old airfield has one of Europe's most extensive collections of historic aeroplanes. As well as products of the once well-developed Czechoslovak aircraft industry, there are Cold War machines from both sides of the Iron Curtain, Soviet Ilyushins, Yaks and Lavochkins, as well as British Meteors and American Phantoms. Prague was one of the places where the German Luftwaffe made a final stand in the last days of World War II, leaving behind examples of the advanced Messerschmitt 262 jet fighter.

ing the founder of the monastery, Peter I of Rosenberg, and *Christ on the Mount of Olives*; and the second from Třeboň (1380–85), whose artist was one of the most important figures of the International Style. Also look out for the series from the Chapel of the Holy Cross at Karlštejn (1360–4) by Master Theodoric.

There then follows some very fine Bohemian woodcarving, especially that of the *Pregnant Virgin Mary* (1430–40) and *St John the Evangelist* (*c.*1400–50) by the Master of the Týn Crucifixion.

Later works are displayed in the long final gallery. Prominent here are some rather gruesome depictions of the Crucifixion; also look for the *St James Cycle*, with souls being dragged from people's mouths and some fierce demons. Influence

89

from the Netherlands can be seen in Hans Pleydenwurff's *Beheading of St Barbara* (c.1470), and, at the end of the 15th century, from the Italian Renaissance in the work of the Master of Grossgmain.

As well as some fabulous Swabian and Bohemian woodcarving, there are two excellent paintings by Lucas Cranach the elder (the *Madonna of Poleň*, 1520, and *Young Lady with a Hat*, 1538). The galleries end with a display of woodcuts, notably Dürer's *Apocalypse* (1511) and the series *The Passion Cycle* (1509) by Cranach.

Smetana Museum (Muzeum B. Smetany)

Novotného lávka 1; tel: 222 220 082; Wed–Mon 10am–noon, 12.30–5pm; admission charge; tram: 17, 18, 53, metro: Straroměstská; map p.134 A3

On a small spit of land, just south of the Charles Bridge, is the Smetana Museum, dedicated to the nationalist composer Bedřich Smetana (1824–84). Housed in a neo-Renaissance former municipal waterworks, the museum illustrates the life and work of the father of Czech music with scores, diaries, manuscripts, and his personal paraphernalia.

Nové Město

Alfons Mucha Museum

Kaunický palác, Panská 7; tel: 224 216 415; www.mucha.cz; daily 10am–6pm; admission charge; tram: 3, 9, 14, 24, metro: Můstek; map p.134 C3

A master of the Art Nouveau style, Alfons Mucha (1860–1939) rose to fame for his posters of actor Sarah Bernhardt. A selection of these is displayed in this small

museum, as well as a number of his paintings and sketchbooks, and memorabilia from his studio in Paris.

Dvořák Museum (Muzeum Antonína Dvořáka)

Ke Karlovu 20; tel: 224 923 363; www.nm.cz; Apr–Sept Tue–Fri 10am–1.30pm, 2–5.30pm, Oct–Mar 9.30am–1.30pm, 2–5pm; admission charge; metro: I.P. Pavlova; map p.136 C2

The Villa Amerika houses a museum dedicated to one of the Czech Republic's greatest composers, Antonín Dvořák (1841–1904). This charming little building, named after a 19th-century inn and designed by Kilián Ignaz Dientzenhofer, was constructed in 1717–20 as a summer palace for the prominent Catholic Michna family.

Inside, the museum contains various Dvořák memorabilia, including his Bösendorfer piano and viola, as well as displays of photographs and facsimiles of letters, tickets and manuscripts. On the first floor is a beautifully decorated little concert hall where recitals are sometimes given.

Left: view from the Smetana Museum. **Right:** the National Museum.

Although the labelling is in Czech, a guide in English can be borrowed from the front desk.

Mánes Exhibition Space (Výstavní síň Mánes)
Masarykovo nábřeží 250; tel: 224 930 754; Tue–Sun 10am–6pm; admission charge; www.nadace-cfu.cz; tram: 17, 21; map p.136 A1

The Mánes Exhibition Space is an excellent example of Functionalist architecture built for the Mánes Association of Fine Artists in 1927–30 and designed by Otakar Novotný. It is now run by the Foundation Czech Art Fund and is used to hold temporary exhibitions of contemporary art.

National Museum (Národní muzeum)
Václavské náměstí 68; tel: 224 497 111; www.nm.cz; daily May–Sept 10am–6pm, Oct–Apr 9am–5pm, closed first Tue of the month; admission charge; tram: 11, metro: Muzeum; map p.136 C1

Constructed between 1885 and 1890 to designs by Josef Schulz, this neo-Renaissance palace houses collections of natural and national history, as well as a large library. It is worth a quick visit, not so much for the exhibitions – which are used mainly to bore parties of schoolchildren – but for the lavish design of the grand entrance foyer, dignified with busts of famous Czechs.

Police Museum
Ke Karlovu 1; tel: 224 922 183; Tue–Sun 10am–5pm; admission charge; tram: 6, 11, metro: IP Pavlova; map p.136 C3

Housed in a 14th-century monastery, this eccentric collection contains everything from the bizarre to the banal. The Hall of the Traffic Branch of the Czech Police Force, with its dressed dummies, is comically dull, while The Centre for Road Accident Prevention is just dull. The sections on murders is macabre to say the least, while the displays on counter-espionage and Iron Curtain border patrols are fascinating.

Prague City Museum (Muzeum hlavního města Prahy)
Na Poříčí 51; tel: 224 223 696; www.muzeumprahy.cz; Tue–Sun 9am–6pm; admission charge; metro: Florenc; map p.135 D2

Despite the unpromising location, this is a fascinating museum set in an imposing building. Much of the labelling is in Czech only, so ask to borrow the English booklet from the front desk.

The galleries take you through the history of the city in great depth, from prehistory and the medieval period on the ground floor, to the Renaissance and Baroque upstairs. The gallery on the Renaissance is particularly interesting, dealing with the reign of Rudolf II and his team of alchemists; it has also been given a very attractive painted and beamed ceiling.

However, the museum's prize exhibit is undoubtedly Antonín Langweil's enormous

Left: Alfons Mucha Museum. **Right:** Police Museum.

paper model of the city made in 1826–37. This shows the streets and buildings in phenomenal detail, making it possible to trace your present-day wanderings along the early 19th-century street pattern. Also here is Josef Mánes's original design for the astrological face of the Old Town Hall clock.

Smíchov and the Southwest

Mozart Museum (Muzeum W.A. Mozarta Bertramka)

Mozartova 169; tel: 257 318 461; www.bertramka.com; open daily Apr–Oct 9am–6pm, Nov–Mar 9.30am–4pm; admission charge; tram: 6, 9, 12, 20, metro: Anděl

This picturesque villa was where Mozart stayed on his visits to Prague in 1787 and 1791. It now operates as a museum dedicated to Prague's musical life at the time. The first room has a cabinet of instruments, including an early clarinet and a basset horn – which Mozart was chiefly responsible for introducing to the orchestra.

In the next room is a real piece of Mozartiana, an elegant fortepiano by Ignatz Kober (Vienna, 1785–6), one of only three such instru-

ments to survive. Legend has it that Mozart played on this instrument in Prague in January 1787. Close by is a hammer piano (1807–10) used in the filming of *Amadeus*. To complete the trio of keyboard instruments, towards the end of the exhibition is a large harpsichord, made in 1722, and the only surviving example by Johann Heinrich Gräbner of Dresden.

The museum's walls are lined with illustrations and documents, which build up an interesting picture of Prague during Mozart's time. On the more kitsch side is a small glass tablet encasing a lock of Mozart's hair. You can also see photographs of the numerous famous musical visitors – Tchaikovsky, Vin-

cent d'Indy, Leoš Janáček – who later came to pay homage at this Mozart shrine on their visits to Prague.

The villa regularly holds concerts of Mozart's music (see the website for details), at which times the museum café opens late especially.

Holešovice and Troja

Lapidarium

Výstaviště 422; tel: 233 375 636; www.nm.cz; currently closed for renovation; tram: 5, 12, 14, 15, 17

To the right of the Průmyslový palác, in one of the side pavilions, is the National Museum's Lapidarium. This, the Bohemian stone-sculpture collection of the 11th to 19th centuries, contains some of the most important statues that at one time decorated the city. The Lapidarium is currently closed for – in that common Czech term – 'technical reasons', and there are no hints as to when it will reopen; keep your eye on the website for further information.

However, the items the museum holds are well worth a look when it does reopen. Among the Romanesque and Gothic exhibits, one of the finest is the original of the bronze equestrian statue of St George, which originally stood outside St Vitus's (now replaced by a copy). Also here is the original tympanum from the Týn Church (1380–90), Petr Parléř's exceptional figures from the Old Town Bridge Tower, as well as the original pillar and statue of the *Bruncvík*.

The Renaissance exhibits are dominated by the Krocín

Left: Mozart Museum.

(1865–98) depicts *The Battle of Lipany, 1434*, from the Hussite Wars.

National Gallery of Modern Art (Veletržní Palác)
Dukelských hrdinů 47; tel: 224 301 024; www.ngprague.cz; Tue–Sun 10am–6pm; admission charge; tram: 5, 12, 14, 15, 17, metro: Vltavská

The 'Trade Fair Palace' is one of the earliest large-scale Functionalist buildings in Europe. It was built in 1925–9 and designed by Oldřich Tyl and Josef Fuchs to house exhibitions to show off Czech industrial expertise. It was admired by Le Corbusier, who saw in it how his own large-scale projects might be realised, while qualifying his enthusiasm by saying, 'It's an interesting building but it's not yet architecture.' It was used for industrial exhibitions until 1951, and then as the offices for several foreign trade companies until 1974, when it was badly damaged in a fire. Rebuilt in 1995, it now houses the National

fountain that used to stand in Staroměstské náměstí. And the Baroque pieces include the original (earlier) equestrian statue of St Wenceslas from Václavské náměstí, as well as a series of interesting gilded and brightly painted statues.

The remainder of the collection is given over to works from the 19th century. Notable among these are the two tombs made by Václav Prachner, and the four allegorical groups designed for the cupola of

the National Museum by Bohuslav Schnirch.

Marold Panorama
Výstaviště; Apr–Oct Tue–Fri 2–5pm, Sat–Sun 10am–5pm; admission charge; tram: 5, 12, 14, 15, 17

Behind the now partially destroyed main exhibition hall at Výstaviště is the restored Panorama. Panoramas were very popular during the 19th century – especially of subjects that portrayed patriotic themes – and this huge circular painting by Luděk Marold

Gallery's collections of 19th-, 20th- and 21st-century art.

At the time of writing, however, the permanent exhibition was undergoing reorganisation, with the 19th-century Czech collection (though not the French collection) being transferred from the fourth floor here to St George's Convent in Hradčany. The route around the museum described below should, even so, still be valid.

CZECH ART 1900–1930
Begin your visit on the third floor. The first galleries here are given over to František Kupka (1871–1957), who worked in a range of styles, from symbolist to Fauvist to abstract. Next are the experimental photographic works of František Drtikol (1883–1961), with their Art Deco feel. Then there is the Cubism at which Czech artists so excelled. Look out for Emil Filla's *Salome* (1911–12) and the unsurpassed Cubist furniture and ceramics of Josef Gočar (1880–1945) and Pavel Janák

(1882–1956). In fact, many of the most interesting exhibits in this section of the museum relate more to design than high art. There are many fascinating works in the genres of book illustration, stage design, fashion, architecture, aircraft design and furniture. Look out, in particular, for the models, drawings and photographs of the architects Aldolf Loos and Ludvík Kysela.

FRENCH ART
The highlight of the museum for many people will be the galleries of French art, also on the third floor. Thanks to state acquisitions of major collections in 1923 and 1960, and numerous individual acquisitions in between, hardly any major French painter from the mid-19th to the early 20th century is not represented here.

The displays begin with some busts by Rodin, three small pictures by Delacroix, a couple by Corot and several particularly fine works by Courbet, notably *Woman in a*

Straw Hat with Flowers (1857) and *Forest Grotto* (c.1865). Next are the Impressionists, well represented with paintings by Pissarro, Sisley and Monet. There are also some interesting daubs by Degas and Renoir.

Look out, also, for Toulouse-Lautrec's picture of two women dancing together, *At the Moulin Rouge* (1892), some fine examples of Gauguin's work

Clockwise from left: works by František, Filla and Loos.

(especially *Flight*, 1902), and Van Gogh's vibrant canvas *Green Wheat* (1889). Perhaps most impressive of all, though, is the group of 19 works by Picasso, from the early *Seated Female Nude* (1906) to a wide range of his Cubist paintings.

ART FROM 1930 TO THE PRESENT DAY

The collections on the second floor begin with an exhibition on cinema and theatre. There is also a display celebrating the work of the master puppeteer and animator Jiří Trnka (1912–69), sometimes described as the 'Disney of the East'.

Succeeding galleries chart the Czech contribution to Surrealism, with works by Jindřich Štyrský (1899–1942), by the female artist who went under the name of Toyen (1902–80), and by Zdeněk Pešánek (1896–1965), who produced extraordinary illuminated sculptures.

The grimness of the wartime occupation is expressed in works by the

artists of Group 42. Works such as *Railroad Station with a Windmill* by František Hudeček (1909–) combine the artistic innovations of the previous decades with a fascination with industry and technology.

The post-war landscape looked hardly less optimistic. After 1948, Socialist-Realism was the only recognised artistic creed. Art became divided into the official and unofficial, and any artists deemed to be either 'individualists' or 'formalists' were driven underground. There is a small display of Socialist-Realist paintings (most of the gallery's holdings of art of this type languish in disgrace in store). Then there are much larger spaces devoted to artists who worked outside the official ideology.

20TH-CENTURY FOREIGN ART

On the first floor is the collection of Foreign Art, which has particular strength and depth in Austrian and German Expressionist art. Here you can find paintings by Max Oppenheimer, Egon Schiele and Oskar Kokoschka. There are also the important, earlier, proto-Expressionist works by

Edvard Munch: *Dancing on a Shore* (1900) and *Seashore Landscape near Lübeck* (1907).

Moving on, there are fine Secessionist works by Gustav Klimt, Cubist-inspired paintings by Aristarkh Lentulov, and Paul Klee's mesmerising *Tropical Forest* (1915). Thereafter, the collection is patchy in its continuation of the story of 20th-century art. Although there are pieces by Miró and Picasso, Henry Moore, Joseph Beuys and Antoni Tàpies, the quality of the collection is uneven.

Finally, if you have time to spare, visit one of the temporary exhibitions else-

Left and below: City Transport Museum.

including helicopters, biplanes, hot-air balloon baskets and the tiny Nebeská Belcha plane from 1937. Other galleries display clocks, astronomical instruments, gramophones, photographic equipment, movie projectors and even Charlie Chaplin's bowler hat, cane and gloves. The basement contains an extraordinary recreation of a coal mine (guided tours are available in English).

Villa Bílek

Mickiewiczova 1; tel: 224 826 391; www.citygalleryprague.cz; currently closed for renovation; trams 18, 22, 57

This striking building houses a museum of the works of Czech symbolist and Art Nouveau sculptor František Bílek. The house, which dates from 1911, was designed by the artist to create, in his own words, 'a workshop and a temple'. The interior of the villa

where in the museum. Recent offerings have included the triennial show of contemporary art and a selection of Modigliani's finest works.

National Technical Museum (Národni Technické Muzeum)

Kostelní 42; tel: 220 399 111; www.ntm.cz; Tue–Fri 9am–5pm, Sat–Sun 10am–6pm; admission charge; tram: 1, 8, 15, 25, 26, metro: Hradčanská, Vltavská; map p.134 B1

Situated on the northern edge of Letná Park, the Technical Museum charts Czechoslovakia's impressive record in science and technology. It is currently undergoing renovation, and will reopen, section by section, from 2009 onwards. The Transport Hall has steam trains, vintage motorcycles and bicycles, cars, fire-engines and model ships. There is also a wonderful collection of flying machines,

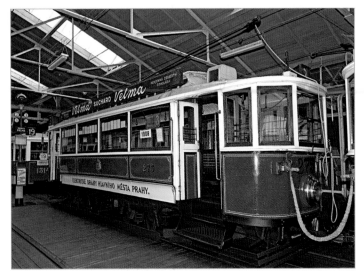

Right: statues outside the Villa Bilek.

makes much use of rough-hewn stone, arches and niches. Unfortunately, little of the original furniture remains, but that which does is very attractive, especially the Cubist sideboard of 1910.

Although it is currently being restored, the museum holds good examples of the sculptor's work; much of it is religious in inspiration, with a strong emphasis on struggle and suffering (for example, *Grief*, 1908–9).

One of the most interesting exhibits is the large plaster model for the *National Monument for the White Mountain*, which was planned for the 300th anniversary of the battle in 1920. Bilek submitted a design after an initial proposal from Stanislav Sucharda was poorly received. This would have been his largest project, and very spectacular. However, in the end the project was not realised, ostensibly due to lack of funding, and the commemoration had to make do with the small mound and plaque that can still be seen at the site.

Bubeneč, Střešovice and Břevnov

City Transport Museum (Muzeum městské hromadné dopravy)
Patočkova 4, tel: 296 124 900; www.dpp.cz; 22 Mar–17 Nov Sat–Sun 9am–5pm; admission charge; tram: 1, 2, 15, 18, 25; map p.132 A1
The City Transport Museum is, as should be hoped, easily reached by public transport from the city centre. Set in an old tram shed, this is also where the 'nostalgic' tram 91 begins and ends its journey *(see box, below for details)*. The museum comprises a collection of trams and trolleybuses and demonstrates the history of public transport in the city. The exhibits range from a horse-drawn tram car dating from 1886 to a bus dating from

Every year the Transport Museum runs one of its old trams along a route through the city centre, taking in a number of Prague's main sights. Numbered as **Tram 91**, the route varies slightly each year, but generally it runs from the museum in Střešovice to the Výstaviště exhibition ground via Malá Strana, the National Theatre, Wenceslas Square and Náměstí republicky. The trip takes about 40 mins, leaving on the hour from midday, there is a 20-min wait and then the tram makes its way back again to the Transport Museum (see www.dpp.cz for more details).

1985. Some of the early trams are beautifully made and decorated in Art Nouveau style, and there is an interesting exhibition showing the building of the city's metro.

Vinohrady and Žižkov

Museum of Military History (Vojenský Historický Ústav Praha)
U památníku 2; tel: 973 204 913; www.vhu.cz; Tue–Sun 9.30am–6pm; free; bus: 133
Located just off the path up the the National Monument, the city's Museum of Military History is rather more interesting than first impressions of its grim Modernist concrete exterior might suggest. The exhibits tell the story of the Czechoslovak Army from its inception in 1918 up to World War II and, apart from an impressive collection of headwear, there are good displays on the role played by Czech troops in World Wars I and II.

97

M

Music

Prague is unquestionably a city of music. The violinist David Oistrakh once described it as the 'musical heart of Europe', and the city is still the centre of Bohemia's rich musical heritage, as it has been for centuries. The great flowering of Czech music, also known as Bohemian classicism, took place in the 18th century. When the English composer Charles Burnley visited Bohemia in 1772, he was so surprised by the level of musical skill in the country that he named it the 'conservatory of Europe'. This stems from Bohemia's traditional patronage of music and support for musical education.

Classical Music

As part of the Habsburg Empire, Prague was initially open to musical influence from the German-speaking world. The most famous of those composers who visited the city was **Wolfgang Amadeus Mozart** (1756–91). Mozart left his home town of Salzburg, Austria, to build a career for himself in Vienna, but the Viennese public and the court did not always appreciate him. His opera *The Marriage of Figaro* had, however, been enthusiastically received in Prague. An invitation to visit the city followed, and he came to the city in 1787.

He received a commission for an opera from the impresario of what was then the Nostitz Theatre (now the **Estates Theatre**). In contrast to other theatres in Central Europe, the Nostitz was not tied to a court, but was a relatively independent institution. The Prague premiere of **Don Giovanni** in the autumn of 1787, conducted by Mozart himself, was an unprecedented success.

The German influence

From the early 19th century on, the aristocracy of Prague gradually lost their position as the most important patrons of the arts. The rising middle classes claimed their share in the process of shaping cultural life. The centre of activity moved from aristocratic salons to public concert halls, and a new era dawned. It was shaped by two institutions which both left a definitive mark. One was the **Society of Artists**, founded in 1803 and modelled on its predecessor in Vienna; the other was the **Prague Conservatory**, which opened in 1811. This was the first in Central Europe, and set the standard for the rest.

Carl Maria von Weber, director of the Nostitz Theatre from 1813–16, acquainted Prague with Beethoven's *Fidelio*, and the first Romantic operas and Beethoven concerts took place in the Konvikt, a complex in Bartolomějská (now the Czech Film Archive). Later in the 19th century, a concert hall on the Slovanský ostrov became a venue for Berlioz, Wagner and Liszt.

Left: performance at the State Opera house.

Left: the Estates Theatre, where Don Giovanni premiered.

York Conservatory, and his Ninth Symphony, *From the New World*, had a distinctly Slavonic flavour.

Dvořák could be said to be the founder of a musical dynasty. His daughter, Otilka, married the Czech violinist, composer and student of Dvořák Josef Suk (1874–1935), whose grandson, also called Josef, is a famous modern violinist. The grandfather was co-founder of the Bohemia Quartet and is now remembered for his fine orchestral works.

Janáček and Martinů

The two figures that dominated Czech music during the first half of the 20th century were **Leoš Janáček** (1854–1928) and **Bohuslav Martinů** (1890–1959). Janáček spent almost all his life in Brno, Moravia, and was little-known in Prague until his opera *Jenůfa* was performed in the city in 1916. His music is known for its use of traditional Czech song and, in his operas, for his 'speech-song', that he modelled closely on the cadences of the Czech language. Although most of his works were premiered in Brno, after 1916 they were all quickly repeated in Prague, and he became an important figure in the creation of a national cultural identity around the time of the emergence of the Czechoslovak state.

Martinů was similarly drawn to using traditional Czech music in his works, but he was also influenced by developments in contemporary French music. He went to Paris to study with Albert Roussel, initially to escape from the overbearing influence

Bedřich Smetana

The awakening of Czech nationalism during the early 19th century saw a generation of Czech artists faced with the task of reinventing their identities. In music this was to be the great achievement of Bedřich Smetana (1824–84). Born in Litomyšl, Smetana came to the city to study music. He took part in the unsuccessful revolution of 1848, which shaped his desire to unite his artistic expectations with the demands of an independent national culture, eventually realised in his operas. Success came in 1866 with his opera *The Bartered Bride* (1866), after which he became conductor to the Czech Opera and achieved widespread recognition.

After the loss of his hearing in 1874, Smetana gave up his career as a practising musician, but he continued to compose and created some notable works, including the symphonic poem *Má vlast* (My Homeland) and the string quartet *Aus meinem Leben* (From My Life). Smetana

received the highest honour when his opera *Libuše* was performed at the official opening of the National Theatre.

Antonín Dvořák

While everyone in Prague was raving about Smetana, another Czech composer had already started to show his talent. Antonín Dvořák (1841–1904) was born at Nelahozeves, a village near Prague, and first attracted attention with his *Hymnus*, a nationalistic cantata based on Halek's poem *The Heroes of the White Mountain*. He attended the organ school in Prague, played in the National Theatre orchestra, and was organist at St Adalbert's 1874–7.

His talent was recognised by Brahms, who introduced his music to Vienna, sponsoring the publication of the *Klänge aus Mähren* (Sounds from Moravia), which was followed by a commissioned work, *Slavonic Dances*. His *Stabat Mater*, performed in London in 1883, won him European acclaim. In 1892–5 he was director of the New

Left: Agharta Jazz Centrum.

of Czech nationalism. In Paris he encountered Stravinsky, who persuaded him that Czech traditions could be convincingly incorporated into his compositions, and, after a flirtation with neoclassicism, he developed a distinctive and uniquely Czech personal style.

One further composer of the 1930s who must be mentioned is **Vitezslava Kaprálová** (1915–40). Her brief but exceptionally promising career produced several forward-looking and interesting works, including the *Six Variations of the Bells of St Etienne du Mont in Paris* and the *Military Symphonietta*.

Modernists

The strength of national culture did not, however, have a detrimental effect on Prague's open-minded attitude to musical developments occurring elsewhere in Europe. The 1908 premiere of *Symphony 7* by **Gustav Mahler** took place in Prague; in 1885 he had been conductor of the New German Theatre's orchestra. The same orchestra was directed from 1911–27 by **Alexander von Zemlinsky**, who acted as a go-between with the great musical cities, Vienna and Berlin; **Alban Berg** (1885–1935) and **Arnold Schoenberg** (1874–1951)

both visited Prague, and Schoenberg's *Ewartung* was premiered in the city.

The avant-garde were heavily circumscribed during the period of communist rule, yet many of the Czech Republic's most prominent contemporary composers began their careers during this period. Of these one of the most prominent was **Petr Eben** (1929–2007), particularly noted for his works for organ. The Prague-based group of composers known as **Quattro** (Sylvie Bodorová, born 1954, Luboš Fišer, 1935–99, Zdeněk Lukáš, 1928–2007, and Otmar Mácha, 1922–2006) have produced many interesting works. A good source of information on contemporary music in Prague is the Czech Music Information Centre (www.musica.cz).

Classical Performances

Concerts of classical music, mainly chamber ensembles, are held in many churches and historic buildings. Aimed at tourists, the standard is not always high and the repertory very predictable. However, there are some other venues putting on exceptional concerts.

The **Czech Philharmonic** is one of the world's great orchestras, and seeing one of its concerts at the Rudolfinum is a real event.

The other major resident orchestra is the **Prague Symphony Orchestra**. Less well known than the **Czech Philharmonic** but still excellent, it puts on concerts in the Obecní dům from September to June. A third orchestra, the **Prague Radio Symphony Orchestra**, is also resident in the city. Although primarily a recording ensemble, it puts on a fine concert series in the Rudolfinum between October and March.

One of the highest-profile chamber ensembles is the **Suk Chamber Orchestra**. It tends to concentrate on the core Czech repertory. Two orchestras established since 1989 and starting to make an international name for themselves are the **Prague Philharmonia** and the **Czech National Symphony Orchestra**.

Opera and Ballet

The quality of opera performances in Prague is high. Most opera is sung in its original language with digital surtitles in Czech. (Performances in Czech, of works by Dvořák and Smetana for example, do not have subtitles in foreign languages, however.)

The **National Theatre Ballet** frequently performs ballet classics such as *Swan Lake* and *Coppélia*, but has been branching out in more adventurous directions in recent years by including choreographies by George Balanchine and Jiří Kylián. The **Ballet Company of the Prague State Opera** is a relatively new, medium-sized company, incorporating the Prague Chamber Ballet.

Right: performance at the Prague State Opera.

Classical Music and Dance Venues

Duncan Centre
Branická 41, Prague 4; tel: 244 461 342; www.duncanct.cz; tram: 3, 16, 17, 21
This is a popular centre for the teaching and performance of modern dance, and often hosts visiting foreign artists.

Estates Theatre (Stavovské divadlo)
Ovocný trh; tel: 224 215 001; www.estatestheatre.cz; metro: Můstek; map p.134 B3
The theatre where *Don Giovanni* was premiered in 1787, conducted by Mozart himself. His operas are still regularly staged here. Part of the National Theatre network.

National Theatre (Národní divadlo)
Národní třída 2; tel: 224 901 448; www.narodni-divadlo.cz; metro: Národní Třída; map p.134 A4
Opera, ballet and theatre performed by the National Theatre ensembles. This is also the location of the Laterna magika **Black Light Theatre**.
SEE ALSO LITERATURE AND THEATRE, P.76, 77

Obecní dům
Náměstí Republiky 5; tel: 222 002 336; www.obecnidum.cz; metro: Náměstí Republiky; map p.134 C3
This Art Nouveau building has one of the best concert halls in the city and is home to the Prague Symphony Orchestra (www.fok.cz).
SEE ALSO ARCHITECTURE, P.28

Rudolfinum
Náměstí Jana Palacha; tel: 227 059 227; metro: Staroměstská; map p.134 A2

This is the home of the Czech Philharmonic (www.ceska filharmonie.cz) and the Prague Radio Symphony Orchestra (www2.rozhlas.cz/socr). The main concert season runs Oct–May.

Státní Opera Praha
Wilsonova 4; tel: 224 227 266; www.opera.cz; metro: Muzeum; map p.135 C4
Productions here are usually of a very high standard. The repertory provides a mix of 19th-century opera and more daring contemporary works.

Jazz Clubs

Agharta jazz centrum
Železná 16; tel: 222 211 275; www.agharta.cz; metro: Staroměstská; map p.134 B3
A good place to catch top local musicians, and it organises an ongoing jazz festival, attracting classy foreign bands.

Charles Bridge Jazz Club
Saská 3; tel: 257 220 820; www.jazzblues.cz; metro: Malostranská; map p.134 D2
A new, small club in Malá Strana that has a good list of local talent. Music starts at about 9pm and booking a table is advised. Unusually for a Prague club, it is non-smoking.

Jazz lounge U staré paní
Michalská 9; tel: 603 551 680; www.jazzlounge.cz; metro: Staroměstská; map p.134 B3
This 100-seat club draws in some of the best musicians from the Czech Republic and abroad.

U Malého Glena
Karmelitská 23; tel: 257 531 717; www.malyglen.cz; tram:

12, 20, 22, 23; map p.133 C2
Intimate (read tiny) basement that is home to some of the finest jazz in Prague. Good acoustics and a decent bar add to the attractions.

Ungelt Jazz & Blues Club
Týn 2; tel: 224 895 748; metro: Staroměstská; map p.134 B3
A young club with lots of funk and blues aimed at tourists and a cosy stone interior. The programme can be seen online at www.prague.tv.

CD Shops

Bontonland Megastore
Václavské náměstí 1; el: 224 225 277; www.bontonland.cz; Mon–Sat 9am–8pm, Sun 10am–7pm; metro: Můstek; map p.134 B4

Via Musica
Malostranské náměstí 13; tel: 257 535 568; www.viamusica.cz; daily 10.30am–6pm; tram: 212, 20, 22, 23; map p.133 C2

Musical life in Prague has never been restricted to classical music, and its jazz and rock scenes have long had a reputation for lively invention, and have played a significant part in political dissent. Jazz arrived early in Prague. Home-grown talent soon emerged, most importantly in the orchestra led by Jaroslav Ježek during the 1930s at the Gramoklub. Jazz was banned by the Nazis but emerged again, within limits, under the communist regime, particularly after Stalin's death. One of the most influential groups of this time was Studio 5. With the clampdown following the Prague Spring, the radical musical mantle passed to rock, in particular the Plastic People of the Universe, formed in 1968. It was the suppression of this group that led to the setting up of the human rights petition Charter 77.

Nightlife

Although Prague may not be as hip as Berlin or Barcelona and is still in thrall to techno, you only need to take a short ride on a night tram: to see that Praguers know how to have a big night out. This chapter covers cocktail and DJ bars, dance clubs, and gay and lesbian venues. For information about what's on, look out for the flyers and free listings booklets in bars. If you really are into techno, the website www.techno.cz lists places to check out. For jazz venues see *Music (p.101)*. For more pubs, consult *Cafés and Bars (p.30–33)*.

Clubs

Celnice
V celnici 4; tel: 224 212 240; Sun–Thur 11am–2am, Fri–Sat 11am–4am; admission charge; tram: 5, 8, 14, 51, 54, metro: Náměstí Republiky; map p.134 C3
Underneath the New Town restaurant and bar of the same name, this is still one of Prague's best places for a night out. Very popular, with a well-dressed crowd.

La Fabrique
Uhelný trh 2; tel: 224 233 137; www.lafabrique.cz; Mon–Thur 11–3am, Fri until 4am, Sat–Sun 5pm–4am; admission charge; tram: 6, 9, 18, 21, 22, 23, 51, 54, 57, metro: Můstek, Národní Třída; map p.134 B3
Upstairs is a lively bar with a wide range of drinks. Downstairs, however, is a disco popular with locals and tourists who enjoy cheesy pop tunes.

Mecca
U průhonu 3; tel: 283 870 522; www.mecca.cz; Fri–Sat 10pm–6am; admission charge; tram: 1, 3, 5, 12, 25, 54

Large and flash, the Mecca attracts local DJs and packs club-goers in for techno party nights. Now with jazz nights courtesy of Jazz Club Železná.

Radost FX
Bělehradská 120; tel: 224 254 776; www.radostfx.cz; Mon–Sat 11am–1am, Sun 10.30am–midnight; admission charge; tram: 6, 11, metro: IP Pavlova; map p.137 C2
Still the king of dance clubs, with a good crowd and top local and international DJs playing lots of house and

Left: a night at Roxy.

Cocktail Bars

Alcohol Bar
Dušní 6; tel: 224 811 744; daily 7pm–3am; free; tram: 17, 53, metro: Staroměstská; map p.134 B2

One of a rash of swish cocktail bars in this part of town. There is a staggering range of booze, all beautifully mixed, and the table service is useful as you start to go cross-eyed.

Bugsy's
Pařížská 10; tel: 224 810 287; daily 7pm–2am; free; tram: 17, 53, metro: Staroměstská; map p.134 B3

The original Prague cocktail bar, and still up there with the best. The drinks are expensive but extremely well prepared – taken from their 'Blue Bible' drinks list, offering over 200 choices – and it continues to pull in local celebrities.

Hapu
Orlická 8; tel: 222 720 158; Mon–Sat 6pm–2am; free; tram: 11, 16, 51, 58, metro: Flora

Sink into one of the squishy sofas in this cosy cellar bar in Žižkov and enjoy an expertly mixed cocktail in a relaxed atmosphere.

Getting back late at night is entertainment in itself. The metro closes at about midnight and reopens at 5am. In between those times, your best option is to take a tram or a bus. Any tram with a number in the 50s is a night tram. Night buses are nos. 501 to 512.

R'n'B. The restaurant serves good vegetarian food (excellent for Sunday brunch).

Rock Café
Národní 20; tel: 224 933 947; www.rockcafe.cz; Mon–Sat 5pm–3am, Sun 5pm–1am; admission charge; tram: 6, 9, 18, 21, 22, 23, 51, 54, 57, metro: Národní Třída; map p.134 A4

Music club with bars, venues and dance floors on several levels. The music generally begins from 7.30pm and features everything from DJs to tribute bands to heavy metal.

Roxy
Dlouhá 33; tel: 224 826 296; www.roxy.cz; daily from 7pm,

Left: the gay-friendly Bar 21, *see p.104.*

parties start at 10pm; admission charge; tram: 5, 8, 14, 51, 54; map p.134 B2

One of the biggest clubs in town for house and R&B, attracting big-name foreign DJs. The club also funds the adjoining Galerie NoD, which stages contemporary art shows.

Sedm Vlků
Vlkova 7; tel: 222 711 725; www.sedmvlku.cz; Mon–Sat 5pm–3am; free; tram: 5, 9, 26, 55, metro: Jiřího z Poděbrad; map p.135 E4

One of the best clubs in Žižkov's nightlife central. An excellent sound system draws in music aficionados, and the parties are wildly popular.

Ultramarin
Ostrovní 32; tel: 224 932 249; www.ultramarin.cz; daily 10pm–4am; admission charge; tram: 6, 9, 18, 21, 22, 23, 51, 54, 57, metro: Národní Třída; map p.136 B1

A chic stone cellar that attracts a fashionably older crowd. Upstairs is a decent restaurant-grill serving modern Asian and Pacific Rim dishes.

Ocean Drive

V kolkovně 7; tel: 224 819 089;
daily 4pm–2am; free; tram: 17,
18, 53, metro: Staroměstská;
map p.134 B2

An upmarket cocktail bar
transplanted from Miami to
Prague's Jewish Quarter, this
stylish joint is popular with
local fashionistas and
hangers-on.

Palác Akropolis

Kubelikova 27; tel: 296 330 911;
www.palacakropolis.cz; daily
11am–1am; free; metro: Jiřího z
Poděbrad; map p.135 E4

This Art Deco building in
Žižkov houses an arts centre
featuring a theatre, concert
hall (for indie music gigs), a
cinema and an exhibition
space. There is also a bar-
restaurant on the ground
floor, as well as the Kaaba
Café, Divadelní DJ bar and
Malá Scena, chill-out lounge
elsewhere in the complex.
SEE ALSO LITERATURE AND
THEATRE, P.77

Tretter's

V kolkovně 3; tel: 224 811 165;
www.tretters.cz; free; daily
7pm–3am; tram: 17, 18, 53,
metro: Staroměstská; map
p.134 B2

Gay and lesbian visitors will
encounter few problems in
Prague, which is generally very
safe, even if not entirely out
and proud. An excellent site for
up-to-date information is
http://prague.gayguide.net. The
main lesbian site (all in Czech)
is www.lesba.cz.

A New York-style cocktail bar
with the best drinks in town.
Michael Tretter, the owner,
has won awards for his mix-
ing, and even runs an acad-
emy for bar staff.

U Buldoka

Preslova 353; tel: 257 329 154;
www.ubuldoka.cz; pub:
Mon–Thur 11am–midnight, Fri
until 1am, Sat noon–midnight,
Sun noon–11pm; club:
Mon–Thur 8pm–4am, Fri–Sat
until 5am; free; tram: 6, 9, 12,
20, 58, metro: Anděl

On the ground floor is an old-
fashioned Prague pub serving fine beer and high-carb
Czech food at very reasonable prices. On the level
below is a cocktail bar and
dance floor with DJs every
night from Monday to
Saturday.

Right: the upscale Tretter's.
Below: Palác Akropolis.

U vystřeleného oka

U božich bojovníků 3; tel: 222
540 465; Mon–Sat 4.30pm–
1am; free; tram: 5, 9, 26, 55;
map p.135 E3

Despite plenty of competition,
the Shot-Out Eye is one of the
best pubs in Žižkov. Excellent
beer is served in bizarre and
louche surroundings, all
authentically smoky and generally with loud music playing.
Live jazz every Tue from 8pm.

Gay and Lesbian Venues

Alcatraz

Borivojova 58; tel: 222 711 458;
daily 10pm–5am; admission
charge; tram: 5, 9, 26, 55, 58;
map p.135 E4

Located in Žižkov, this fetish
club and bar has all the facilities and paraphernalia you
could wish for.

Bar 21

Římská 21; tel: 724 254 048;
daily 4pm–4am; free; tram: 11,
metro: Muzeum; map p.137 C1

This mixed gay and lesbian
cellar-bar is popular with the
local scene. Has a laid-back
and friendly atmosphere.

Club TERmix
Třebízského 4a; tel: 222 710 462; www.club-termix.cz; daily 9pm–5am; admission charge; tram: 11, metro: Jiřího z Poděbrad; map p.137 E1
Classy mixed gay and lesbian club with good DJs and a long drinks list. There is also a dark room in which to get to know each other better.

Friends
Bartolomějská 11; tel: 226 211 920; www.friends-prague.cz; daily 6pm–4am; free; tram: 4, 9, 14, 17, 18, 22, 23, 56; metro: Národní Třida; map p.134 A4
Long-established bar with a wide selection of (inexpensive) drinks. Not as lively as it used to be, but a friendly place to start an evening out.

Tingl Tangl
Karolíny Světlé 12; tel: 224 238 278; www.tingltangl.cz; Mon–Sat 8pm–5am; admission charge; tram: 17, 18, 53, metro: Národní Třída; map p.134 A4
A gay, lesbian and straight bar and garden restaurant

with a club downstairs. A drag cabaret is held on Wed, Fri and Sat at 9pm.

Valentino
Vínohradská 40; tel: 222 513 491; www.club-valentino.cz; Thur 8pm–4am, Fri–Sat 9pm–6am; admission charge; tram: 11, metro: Muzeum; map p.137 D1
Large and fun gay club, with all the essentials: two dance floors, chill-out spaces and a dark room 'labyrinth'. The well-designed space is also used for fashion shows.

Right: Friends, a popular gay-friendly bar.

Pampering

While the Czech lands have long been home to famous spas *(see the box on Karlovy Vary, below)*, Prague itself had to wait for spas to arrive in the city itself. These have now been provided by a number of the five-star hotels, and some of these spas are set in historic buildings (including a Renaissance chapel and a Gothic cellar). The treatments on offer include facials from Darphin and Juvena, while there is a large range of massages to choose from. If you are more interesting in acquiring some products to use yourself at home, then visit Botanicus for organic soaps, lotions and oils.

Spas

Ecsotica Spa

Alchymist Grand Hotel, Tržiště 19; tel: 257 286 011; www.alchymisthotel.com; daily 9am–9pm; tram: 12, 20, 22, 23; map p.133 C2

This is a quiet, beautifully decorated little spa set in a Gothic cellar in Malá Strana. Aside from the lovely pool, there are massages, baths, manicures and pedicures, as well as a good range of Darphin facial treatments.

Lily Wellness and Spa

Hotel Hoffmeister, Pod bruskou 7; tel: 724 360 252; www.hoffmeister.cz; book ahead for timings; metro: Malostranská; map p.133 D1

One of the best spas in the city is found in this small luxury hotel. There is a very full list of treatments, which range from massages (including ones with chocolate and honey), Juvena facials and wraps. Perhaps the best, and most relaxing, treatment here, though, is the stone bath: baking-hot volcanic stones are used to create a steam bath in a cave underneath the hotel.

Above: the tranquil lobby at The Spa.

Sabai

Slovanský dům, Na Příkopě 22; tel: 221 451 180; www.sabai.cz; daily 10am–10pm; metro: Můstek; map p.134 B3

This wellness centre specialises in Thai massages, including aromatherapy treatments, massages based on *ayurveda* and even special massages if you are pregnant. The foot massages are particularly good after a long day of sightseeing.

While Prague itself is not traditionally a spa town, **Karlovy Vary** (aka Karlsbad), some 130km (80 miles) to the west of the city, is one of the great European spa centres. During the 19th century the elegant town was fashionable, attracting royalty, artists and the generally very wealthy to its waters. And it is the waters that are the key to its popularity. The resort's springs produce some 3,000 litres (660 gallons) of water a minute, while the Vřídlo – the most famous of these – gives out 3 million litres (660,000 gallons) of water at 70°C (158°F) every day. Among the more famous of the spa's devotees were Goethe and Marx, so perhaps the waters are good for the brain as well as the digestion and liver. (See www.karlovy-vary.cz for more information.)

Left: The Spa at Mandarin
Oriental.

produced organic beauty
products and essential oils.
Most of the ingredients are
sourced from its own organic
botanical gardens in Ostrá,
about 35km (22 miles) from
Prague.

Manufaktura
Melantrichova 17; tel: 221 632
480; www.manufaktura.biz;
daily 10am–8pm; metro:
Staroměstská; map p.134 B3
Better-known for its wooden
toys than beauty products,
Manufaktura also has a range
of traditionally scented home
spa products that are worth
checking out.
SEE ALSO SHOPPING, P.122

Marionnaud Parfumeries
Na Příkopě 19; tel: 272 770 345;
www.marionnaud.cz; Mon–Fri
9am–8pm, Sat 9am–7pm, Sun
11am–7pm; metro: Můstek;
map p.134 B3
Forgotten your favourite
moisturiser or are looking for
make-up or perfume? The
chances are you will find
what you are looking for here,
a large branch of what is
Europe's largest beauty
chain. They stock big-name
brands such as Dior, Guerlain
and Shiseido.

The Spa
Mandarin Oriental, Nebovidská
1; tel: 233 088 880;
www.mandarinoriental.com;
daily 10am–10pm; tram: 12, 22;
map p.133 C3
Claimed to be 'the only spa
in the world located in a former Renaissance chapel',
this is one of the best places
in the country to pamper
yourself. Many of the products are wholly natural, provided by Aromatherapy
Associates. The spa area
itself is large and very relaxing, with a number of private
treatment rooms and suites,
all decorated in a restrained
modern style.

Zen City Spa
Maximilian Hotel, Haštalská 14;
tel: 225 303 116;
www.planetzen.cz; daily
10am–10pm; metro: Náměstí
Republiky; map p.134 B2
One of the first spas in the
city to offer traditional Asian
therapies. The beauticians
are all highly trained, and the
treatments include Thai
massages with exotic oils

and the supremely relaxing
'Bali Blossom' bath full of
flowers and fragrant oils.
They also offer a 'floating'
therapy where you float on
water saturated with salts to
provide buoyancy.

Lotions and Potions
Botanicus
Týn 3; tel: 234 767 446;
www.botanicus.cz; daily
10am–6.30pm; metro:
Staroměstská; map p.134 B3
This delightful and beautifully
smelling shop stocks locally

Right: Zen City Spa,
Maximillian Hotel.

Parks and Gardens

For such a relatively small city, Prague has a surprisingly large amount of open space, whether it is a park, garden or cemetery. Practically every district has a large area of parkland, making it possible, for instance, to walk from Smíchov all the way to Holešovice through adjoining parks and gardens. The larger parks include Petřín Hill, Letná and Stromovka, all on the left bank of the Vltava. Nové Mešto has the University Botanical Gardens, and there is another botanical garden out in Troja.

Malá Strana

Petřín Hill

Malá Strana; daily 24 hours; free; tram 12, 20, 22, 23, 57; map p.132 B3

The park on Petřín Hill was formed by linking up the gardens which had gradually replaced vineyards and a quarry (which provided the stone for the city's buildings). Nowadays, this vast green expanse accommodates orchards (still tended by the monks from the nearby Strahov Monastery), a rose garden, a children's playground, an Eiffel-inspired **Observation Tower**, a mock-Gothic castle containing a **Mirror Maze**, an astronomical **Observatory**, and the so-called **Hunger Wall** (*Hladová zed*), which was commissioned by Charles IV in 1362 as a form of 'New Deal' strategy to provide work for the starving and impoverished.

Access to the park is from Úvoz and the courtyard of the Strahov Monastery in Hradčany (*see p.46*), and Újezd in southern Malá Strana. From the former area you can take the funicular railway up the hill (daily 9am–11.30pm; normal tram and metro tickets are valid).

SEE ALSO CHILDREN, P.40, 41; MONUMENTS, P.80

Vrtba Gardens (Vrtbovská zahrada)

Karmelitská 25; tel: 257 531 480; www.vrtbovska.cz; Apr–Oct daily 10am–6pm; admission charge; tram: 12, 20, 22, 23; map p.133 C2

By the U Malého Glena jazz club is the entrance to the Vrtba Garden. Meticulously restored, these terraced gardens are perhaps the finest example of Baroque landscape in Prague. They feature a *sala terrena* (pavilion) with frescoes by Václav Vavřinec Reiner and a number of sculptures by Matthias Bernhard Braun. The views of the castle hill from the stepped gardens – especially the final terrace – are magnificent.

Wallenstein Gardens

Valdštejnské náměstí 4; tel: 257 072 759; gardens daily Apr–Oct 10am–6pm; free; tram 12, 18, 20, 22, 23, 57, metro Malostranská; map p.133 C2

The gardens of the Wallenstein Palace can be accessed from either Valdštejnské náměstí or Letenská. They were laid out by Italian architects for General Albrecht von Wallenstein (1583–1634) between 1624 and 1630. As things turned out, he only lived in the palace for about a year in total. When he was in residence, he dined in the triple-arched pavilion (*sala terrena*) that overlooks the gardens. This structure is

Wallenstein enlisted under the Habsburg Ferdinand II in the Thirty Years War. He won many victories, became Duke of Mecklenburg, and accumulated great wealth (not least with a grandiose coin swindle). In the end he was able to raise his own private army, the services of which became so expensive that parts of the empire were mortgaged to afford them. He went too far, however, when he hatched a secret deal with the enemy that would eventually have led him to the Bohemian crown. Emperor Ferdinand saw through him: he hired assassins who murdered him in his bed in the town of Cheb in 1634.

Left: Letna Park, *see p.110*.

ovská zahrada, Velká Pálffy-ovská zahrada, Kolowratská zahrada and Malá Fürsten-berská zahrada). The gardens were laid out following the Swedish occupation of the city in 1648 and replaced the Renaissance Italianate gardens that had initially replaced the vineyards that lined the hill. The gardens have been beautifully restored and are full of small follies and statues.

Royal Gardens (Královská zahrada)
Hradčany; tel: 224 373 368; www.hrad.cz; daily Apr, Oct 10am–6pm, May, Sept 10am–7pm, June–July 10am–9pm, Aug 10am–9pm; free; metro: Malostranská; map p.132 C1

The Royal Gardens are on the north side of the castle. To reach them, leave the Second Courtyard by the Picture Gallery, and cross the **Powder Bridge** *(Prašneho mostu)*; the entrance to the gardens is on your right. Famous for their azaleas, they are a lovely place to sit or wander; there is also a modern glasshouse stretching along the side opposite the castle designed by Eva Jiřičná. In the gardens is the **Ball-Game Court** *(Míčovna)*. Built 1565–9 and designed by Bonifác Wohlmut, it has an Italianate sgraffito façade and has recently been restored. At the end of the gardens is the **Summer Palace** *(Belvedér)*, which art historians consider to be the only example of a purely Italian Renaissance building north of the Alps. Emperor Ferdinand I had the palace built in 1537 for his wife Anna. In winter the Belvedér can be reached from Mariánské hradby.

decorated with frescoes of scenes from the Trojan War.

On the western side of the gardens is a large aviary (home to several owls) and an extraordinary artificial grotto with stalactites and grotesques. Elsewhere around the garden are bronze statues of mythological figures – the work of Adriaen de Vries, court sculptor to Emperor Rudolf II. Unfortunately, these are only copies; the originals were taken to Sweden as spoils of war in 1648 and are now in the park of Drottningholm Palace near Stockholm. At the gardens' eastern end is a large ornamental pond and a former Riding School, where temporary exhibitions are held.

SEE ALSO CASTLES, PALACES AND HOUSES, P.34

Hradčany

Gardens on the Ramparts (Zahrada na valech)
Hradčany; daily Apr, Oct 10am–6pm, May, Sept 10am–7pm; June, July 10am–9pm; Aug 10am–8pm; free; metro: Malostranská; map p.132 B1

The Gardens on the Ramparts lie just below the exit from Prague Castle by the Černá věž. About halfway along the path below the castle is the entrance to the Palace Gardens below Prague Castle *(see below)*.

Palace Gardens below Prague Castle (Palácové zahrady pod pražským hradem)
Valdštejnské náměstí 3; tel: 257 010 401; www.palacove zahrady.cz; Apr–Oct daily 10am–6pm; admission charge; metro: Malostranská; map p.133 C2

The Palace Gardens below Prague Castle consist of five separate but linked formal Baroque gardens (the Lede-burská zahrada, Malá Pálffy-

Left: view from the Petřín Hill funicular.

In the park beyond the palace is a large, rather strange, monument in the form of a grotto to Julius Zeyer (1841–1901). Steps below the Belvedér take you down to the tree-lined **Stag Moat** (Jelení příkop). It is possible to return to the U Prašneho mostu by walking up the vale and through a beautifully designed modern tunnel; you can then make your way up to the left.

Nové Město

University Botanical Gardens (Botanické Zahrady University Karlovy v Praze)
Na Slupi 16; tel: 221 951 879; www.natur.cuni.cz; daily Feb–Mar 10am–5pm, Apr–Aug 10am–7.30pm, Sept–Oct 10am–6pm, Nov–Jan 10am–4pm; admission charge for the glasshouse; tram: 18, 24; map p.136 B3

First set out in 1897, and one of the few stretches of greenery in the area, the Prague University Botanical Gardens are delightful; all the specimens are well labelled, and the gardens are dotted with modern sculptures. The winding paths, rockeries and pools mean there are lots of quiet nooks and crannies to explore. The highlight is a beautiful series of restored pre-war greenhouses (slightly earlier closing time than the gardens), dripping with tropical vegetation and including a beautiful lily pond.

Vyšehrad

Vyšehrad Cemetery (Vyšehradský hřbitov)
Vyšehrad; www.hrbitovy.cz; daily Nov–Feb 8am–5pm, Mar–Apr, Oct 8am–6pm, May–Sept 8am–7pm; free; metro: Vyšehrad; map p.136 A4

Vyšehrad Cemetery was created solely to be the final resting place for the country's most revered musicians,

writers and artists. Dominating the cemetery is the tomb of honour known as the **Slavín Monument**, at the end of the main avenue. Two of the most visited graves are those of the two Czech composers Bedřich Smetana and Antonín Dvořák. Dvořák's grave is among the most extravagant in the complex. Also buried here is the 19th-century author of tales of life in Malá Strana, Jan Neruda. Visual artists and painters are represented by the sculptor Josef Myslbek (1848–1929) and Alfons Mucha (1860–1939).

Holešovice to Troja

Letná Park (Letenské sady)
Letná; daily sunrise–sunset; free; metro: Hradčanská; map p.134 A1–B1

Letná Park, a spread of green between Hradčany and Holešovice, was laid out in the mid-19th century, and the views across the city from its southern edge are wonderful. It was on the edge of this escarpment that the enormous statue to Stalin was erected. It was subsequently demolished, and all that remains is its pyramidal granite base, topped with a large metronome by the artist David Černý. The park was also the scene of the largest demonstration of the Velvet Revolution – an irony given that it was also the venue for the communist May Day parades – but is now given over to people cycling, walking dogs and jogging.

On the edge of the park, overlooking the escarpment, are two buildings of interest. The ornate Art Nouveau Hanavský pavilon (now a restaurant) and, further along, the Czechoslovak Pavilion for the Brussels Expo 1958.

Prague Botanical Gardens (Botanická zahrada Praha)
Troja; tel: 603 582 191; www.botanicka.cz; daily Apr 9am–6pm, May–Sept 9am–7pm, Oct 9am–5pm, Nov–Mar 9am–4pm; entrance charge; bus: 112

To reach the gardens, take the footpath that leads off the right from the road that climbs the hill above the Troja Château. A signpost points you towards the 'Botanická zahrada Praha'. At the top turn left to find the main entrance.

The gardens are extensive and include, among other things, a Mediterranean and Japanese garden, medicinal and poisonous plants, as well as a perennial flower bed. Also attached to the garden, cascading down the hill towards the château, is the St Clara vineyard. The view from the top of the hill by the St Clara chapel is lovely.

Following the road up to the left of the main entrance brings you to the curving **Fata Morgana** glasshouse (Tue–Sun, same times as the gardens). Divided into three main sections – semi-desert, tropical rainforest and cloud forest – it is now well established and the plants are flourishing. From the dry zone a subterranean passage leads through a divided pool, one side for the Americas, the other for Africa and Asia, before emerging into the hot and steamy tropics: all very green, with huge tropical butterflies flitting amongst the plants. However, perhaps even more interesting is the cooler cloud-forest room, where jets provide a constant mist of water.

Above the glasshouse, footpaths lead through an attractive woodland with picnic and play areas.

Right: re-enacting battles at Letna Park.

Stromovka

Entrance to the left of Výstaviště; tel: 242 441 593; www. stromovka.cz; daily sunrise–sunset; free; tram: 5, 8, 12, 14, 17

Previously a royal hunting ground, this large wooded park became a public space at the beginning of the 19th century and is one of the most extensive open spaces in the city, beloved of picnicking families, joggers and cyclists.

Břevnov

Divoká Šárka

Nebušice; daily 24 hours; free; metro Dejvická then tram 20, 26

Located to the north of Ruzyně and Břevnov, this wild expanse of parkland – with its woods, rocky outcrops, streams and waterfalls – was originally a hunting ground. Nowadays it is a popular place to walk, jog, cycle, rollerblade and even, when the weather is right, ski cross-country.

In the middle of the park there is a reservoir known as Dzban (literally, 'jug'), which is used for swimming in the summer. In addition, there is a swimming pool, though this is not much warmer as it is fed by a stream. The pool centre also has *pétanque* courts and a football pitch, while nearby is U Veseliku, a pub with a large terrace, selling cool draught beer and grilled sausages. Elsewhere in the park, there is a campsite (tel: 235 358 554; www.campdzban.eu), a golf course (tel: 774 203 729; www.gcds.cz), and a children's playground.

Obora Hvězda Park

Na vypichu; tel: 220 612 229; www.oborahvezda.webpark.cz; daily May–Sept 10am–5pm, Oct–Apr 10am–4pm; entrance charge; tram: 8, 22

The tram stop at Vypich brings you to the edge of the Obora hvězda park. Either walk diagonally across the green to the small gateway, or walk along Na vypichu to the main gate, just where it turns into Libocká (it is also close to the Petřiny tram terminus).

The park, with its tree-lined avenues, was laid out around one of the most interesting Renaissance buildings in the city, the **Letohrádek hvězda**, and the wooded walkways and long avenues make it a very pleasant place to while away a couple of hours.

SEE ALSO CASTLES, PALACES AND HOUSES, P.39

Vinohrady and Žižkov

Havlíček Gardens (Havlíčkovy sady)

Rybalkova; daily sunrise–sunset; free; tram: 4, 22, 23

The Havlíček Gardens, Prague's second-largest park, are a pleasant green space to the south of náměstí Míru. They were once an orchard, and part of the park is still given over to a vineyard. Also here is the **Gröbovka**, a 19th-century villa by the architect Antonín Barvitius.

Olšany Cemetery (Hřbitov Olšany)

Vinohradská; www.hrbitovy.cz; daily Nov–Feb 8am–5pm, Mar–Apr, Oct 8am–6pm, May–Sept 8am–7pm; free; metro: Flora

Olšany Cemetery is a huge necropolis, and was the pre-ferred burial spot of many famous Czechs (particularly if they had not managed to get a spot in Vyšehrad). Wonderfully Gothic in parts, it has higgledy piggledy graves, all slightly overgrown. Among the famous people buried here are Josef Mánes, František Bílek and Josef Lada. However, perhaps the most venerated grave is that of Jan Palach, whose body was moved here in 1990. Palach is buried near the main entrance on Vinohradská.

Reiger Gardens (Riegrovy sady)

Třebízského; daily sunrise–sunset; free; tram: 11; map p.135 D4

Reiger Gardens, this time to the north of náměstí Míru, are a large, well laid-out park along the slopes of the hill, which offers a beautiful view across the whole city right up to Hradčany and the castle. Numerous local pubs with good basic food and beer can be found alongside the park.

Restaurants

Prague restaurants vary enormously in character and price. Bargain meals can be had in some city-centre establishments; following office workers on their way to lunch is one way of discovering them. In addition, visitors should not overlook the numerous sausage stands stationed around the city centre. Czech sausages are among the best in the world and are delicious with a generous dollop of mustard. Another speciality worth looking out for is the open sandwich *(obložené chlebíčky)*, available at delicatessens. Toppings may include slivers of ham, salami, hard-boiled egg, fish roe, potato salad, slices of tomato and gherkins.

Malá Strana

Alchymist
Tržiště 19; tel: 257 286 019; www.alchymisthotel.com; daily noon–3pm, 7pm–11pm; €€€€; tram: 12, 20, 22, 23, 57; map p.132 C2

Decorated in upmarket bordello style, this restaurant is the place to come if you have done rather well out of the post-communist privatisations. If you can afford to ignore the prices, the food and extensive wine list are of a respectable standard.

Gitanes
Tržiště 7; tel: 257 530 163; www.gitanes.cz; daily noon–midnight; €€€; tram: 12, 20, 22, 23, 57; map p.132 C2

Cosy restaurant specialising in the cuisine of the former Yugoslavia. The atmosphere is set by the flowery cloths on the tables and naïve paintings, photographs and farm implements on the walls. The menu completes the sense of nostalgia: home-made bread with paprika milk-fat spread, roasted chips made from salty dough, Javorina schnitzel, lamb sausages, pasta alla Trieste, Yugoslavian cheeses and boiled apples filled with nuts and topped with whipped cream.

Kampa Park
Na Kampě 8b; tel: 296 826 102; www.kampagroup.com; daily 11.30am–1am; €€€; tram: 12, 20, 22, 23, 57; map p.133 D2

The food is good and the views over the river are spectacular. The steep prices, however, may cause some

Left: Hapsburg style still exists, at a price.

Hradčany

Malý Buddha

Úvoz 46; tel: 220 513 894; www.malybuddha.cz; Tue–Sun noon–10.30pm; €–€€; tram: 22, 23; map p.132 B2

Bizarre and incongruous it may be, but this is one of the better-value restaurants in tourist-thronged Hradčany, and a relaxing haven. This candlelit oriental teahouse serves good, mostly vegetarian, food (spring rolls, noodles, Thai curries) as well as numerous varieties of tea, and ginseng wine.

U Císařů

Loretánská 5; tel: 220 518 484; www.ucisaru.cz; daily 11am–midnight; €€€; tram: 22, 23; map p.132 B2

This restaurant's name translates as 'At the Emperor's', and appropriately enough, it is only on the other side of the square from the Castle. The old-fashioned Czech menu includes wild boar, pheasant and duck, though there are, surprisingly, also a few vegetarian dishes.

Staré Město

Allegro

Four Seasons Hotel, Veleslavínova 2; tel: 221 427 000; www.fourseasons.com/prague; daily 7am–11pm; €€€€; tram: 17, 18, 53, metro: Staroměstská; map p.134 A3

Often hailed as the best restaurant in the city, Allegro

Watch the Bill

Prague used to be notorious for the surliness and frequent dishonesty of restaurant staff. The situation has improved considerably, but diners still need to keep a watchful eye on the bill.

Menu prices include value-added tax, but some waiters persist in adding it to the total, and then pocketing it for themselves. In pretentious restaurants, beware of the tray of hors d'oeuvres you may be offered; far from being complimentary, it may add substantially to the bill. Other items such as bread, butter, olives and mayonnaise are also often used to extract more money out of you.

---

indigestion. Popular with local celebrities.

Pálffy Palác

Valdštejnská 14; tel: 257 530 522; www.palffy.cz; daily 11am–11pm; €€€–€€€€; metro: Malostranská; map p.133 D1

Go through the door in the right-hand side of the imposing gateway and up the stairs to reach a dining hall that epitomises faded glory – all gilded chandeliers and yellowing walls. The food is competent but unremarkable, a combination of French and Czech, but it is the surroundings that really count.

U Modré kachničky

Nebovidská 6; tel: 257 320 308; www.umodrekachnicky.cz; daily noon–4pm, 6.30–midnight; €€€; tram: 12, 20, 22, 23, 57; map p.133 C3

This charming Bohemian restaurant serves fine duck and game dishes. Try venison with bilberries and spinach or duck with walnut stuffing. Make sure you save space for the lovely fruit dumplings for dessert.

U Patrona

Dražického náměstí 4; tel: 257 530 725; www.upatrona.cz; daily 10am–midnight; €€€€; metro: Malostranská; map p.133 D2

These elegant dining rooms close to the Charles Bridge are a good place to try some well-prepared Bohemian specialities. Dishes include game consommé with juniper berries and roast goose with red cabbage.

Approximate prices for an average two-course dinner with a glass of house wine per person, including service and tax:

€	under €15
€€	€15–25
€€€	€25–40
€€€€	over €40

Left: Gitanes.

Approximate prices for an average two-course dinner with a glass of house wine per person, including service and tax:

€	under €15
€€	€15–25
€€€	€25–40
€€€€	over €40

was the first recipient of a Michelin star in the whole of post-communist Eastern Europe. Breakfast, lunch and dinner are served either in the dining room, or, during the summer, on the outdoor terrace with its views across the river to the castle. Menus offer a delicious array of well-thought-out dishes, many given an Italian twist courtesy of chef Vito Mollica. Sunday brunch is served 11.30am–3pm.

Ariana

Rámová 6; tel: 222 323 438; www.sweb.cz; daily 11am–11pm; €–€€; tram: 5, 8, 14; map p.134 B2

Strange as it may sound, this Afghan restaurant in an old Prague building proves an excellent formula. The Persian-inspired dishes comprise kebabs, curried vegetables and specialities such as steamed bread stuffed with vegetables. Big mounds of rice accompany most dishes, and you can wash it down with a yoghurt drink or sweet chai.

Arzenal Siam-i-Sam

Valentinská 11; tel: 224 814 099; www.arzenal.cz; daily 10am–midnight; €€; metro: Staroměstská; map p.134 A3

The brainchild of Czech designer Bořek Šípek, the front of the shop sells furniture, glass and ceramics while the back is given over to an excellent Thai restaurant with good service and a stylish interior. The spicy, authentic dishes are beautifully presented – the idea is that you can also buy the dishes and glasses out front – and the large menu includes many vegetarian options.

Brasileiro

U Radnice 8; tel: 224 234 474; www.ambi.cz; daily 11am–midnight; €€; metro: Staroměstská; map p.134 B3

One of the successful Ambiente group of restaurants, the Brasileiro specialises in Uruguayan and Brazilian beef offered on an 'as much as you can eat' formula. Wash your meal down, if you can, with wine from Uruguay.

Country Life

Melantrichova 15; tel: 224 213 373/366; www.countrylife.cz;

Right: Café Flambee.

open Mon–Thur 9am–8.30pm, Fri until 6pm/3pm, Sun 11am–8.30/6pm; €; metro: Můstek; map p.134 B3

Run by the Seventh Day Adventists, this is haven for desperate vegetarians amongst all the butchery proffered everywhere else in Prague. Line up and take what you want from the salad bar and hot dishes (all food is organically grown). When you get to the checkout, your plate is weighed and the cost is calculated.

Dahab

Dlouhá 33; tel: 224 827 375; www.dahab.cz; daily noon–1am; €€; tram: 5, 8, 14, 51, 54; map p.134 B2

An Arab coffee house recreated in central Prague, complete with narghiles, mint tea and couscous. There is a large selection of teas, excellent Turkish coffee and a varied menu of Middle Eastern food, including some good vegetarian dishes.

Don Giovanni

Karolíny světlé 34; tel: 222 222 062; daily 11am–midnight; €€€; tram: 17, 18, 53; map p.134 A3

A long-established Italian restaurant serving surprisingly authentic dishes. There

is also a good range of Italian wines, including one from the owner's vineyard, and some excellent grappa.

Flambée

Betlem Palais, Husova 5; tel: 224 248 512; www.flambee.cz; daily noon–midnight; €€€€; tram: 17, 18, 53; metro: Národní Třída; map p.134 A3

An expensive but high-quality French restaurant that runs a close second to Allegro as the best restaurant in Prague. The rich but beautifully cooked food makes full use of luxury ingredients such as foie gras, truffles and Cognac.

King Solomon

Široká 8; tel: 224 818 752; www.kosher.cz; Sun–Thur noon–11pm; €€€€; tram: 17, 18, 53, metro: Staroměstská; map p.134 A2

The only strictly kosher restaurant in Prague. Hebrew-speaking staff. Among the classic dishes of Central European Jewish cooking are chicken soup, gefilte fish, carp with prunes, and duckling drumsticks with schollet and sautéed cabbage. Kosher wines are from Israel, Hungary, France and the Czech Republic. It is also possible to arrange Shabat meals beforehand and even have them delivered to your hotel.

Klub Architektů

Betlémské náměstí 5a; tel: 224 401 214; daily 11.30am–midnight; €–€€; tram: 17, 18, 53, metro: Národní Třída; map p.134 A3

This place has a bookshop on the ground floor, a gallery first floor and a restaurant in the cellars. The food is generally Mediterranean in style and very good value for money.

Kolkovna

V Kolkovně 8; tel: 224 819 701; www.kolkovna.cz; daily 11am–midnight; €€; tram: 17, 53, metro: Staroměstská; map p.134 B2

Though located in a former printing office in a fine 19th-century building, Kolkovna is a modern take on the traditional beer hall and is licensed from the Pilsner Urquell Brewery. The décor is smart and understated (except for a slightly Captain Nemo copper-plated bar).

The food is solid Czech fare – fried cheese, goulash, roast duck – and reasonably priced.

Le Cornichon

Betlémská 9; tel: 222 211 766; Mon–Sat 4–11pm; €€€; tram: 17, 18, 53, metro: Národní Třída; map p.134 A4

Smart but not starchy restaurant with a modern and well-designed interior. The French-inspired menu is very fairly priced considering the quality of both ingredients and cooking. Start with snail casserole, foie gras or veal sweetbread ravioli. Follow with sea bass with ratatouille, duck with olives and

---

Vegetarians

Vegetarians will find specialist establishments catering to their needs, which is just as well since mainstream restaurants are unlikely to offer them much more than an omelette or fried cheese *(smážený sýr)*; the latter is better than it sounds, consisting of a thick slice of semi-molten local cheese (usually *hermelín*) in a breadcrumb coating and enlivened by a dollop of tartare sauce.

Left: outside at Mala Strana.

turnips or hare à la royale. Finish with a selection of cheeses. Classic French wines are also sold in the associated shop.

Nostress
Dušní 10; 222 317 004; www.nostress.cz; Mon–Fri 8am–11pm, Sat–Sun 10am–11pm; €€€; tram: 17, 53, metro: Staroměstská; map p.134 B2
Stylish café-restaurant with a gallery for contemporary photography attached. The daily lunch menus are reasonably priced (sandwiches and beer are also recommended). Dinner, however, is much more expensive. The well-executed cooking is generally of the fusion cuisine variety.

Obecní dům
Náměstí republiky 5; tel: 222 002 770; www.francouzskarestaurace.cz; Francouzscá restaurace Mon–Sat noon–4pm, 6–11pm, Sun 11.30am–3pm, 6–11pm, Plzeňská restaurace daily 11.30am–11pm, Kavárna Obecní dům daily 7.30am–11pm; €–€€€; metro: Náměstí Republiky; map p.134 C3
Prague's most opulent Art Nouveau building is home to three eateries. The finest – **Francouzscá restaurace** – is an expensive French restaurant offering passable food within a spectacular gilded and chandeliered interior. On the other side of the lobby is the café **Kavárna Obecní dům**, which serves more basic meals and cakes amid equally impressive surroundings. Downstairs in the basement is the cheaper, and smartly decorated, **Plzeňská restaurace**, serving tasty Czech dishes.

Orange Moon
Rámová 5; tel: 222 325 119; www.orangemoon.cz; daily 11.30am–11.30pm; €€; tram: 5, 8, 14; map p.134 B2
This Thai, Burmese and Indian restaurant is housed in a simple tiled cellar. Dishes range from chicken satay and spring rolls to phad thai and fish masala. The food is hot, spicy and tasty.

Pizzeria Rugantino
Dušní 4; tel: 224 815 192; www.rugantino.cz; Mon–Sat 11am–11pm, Sun noon–11pm; €€; tram: 17, 53, metro: Staroměstská; map p.134 B2
Conveniently close to Old Town Square, this restaurant serves large, tasty pizzas at reasonable prices. There is a no-smoking section at the front, overlooking the street, and the staff are friendly.

Potrefená husa
Bílkova 5; tel: 222 326 626; www.potrefenahusa.com; daily 11am–midnight; €€; tram: 17, 53; map p.134 B2
Situated in the basement of one of Prague's Cubist buildings, the 'Shot Goose' appeals to the younger generation of diners with a well-designed interior, moderate prices, updated Czech dishes and a good choice of drinks. It is one of a successful chain, with other branches around the city.

Left: Obecní dům, home of three restaurants..

U medvídků

Na perštýně 7; tel: 224 211
916; www.umedvidku.cz;
Mon–Sat 11.30am–11pm, Sun
11.30am–11pm; €€; metro:
Národní Třída; map p.134 B4
This traditional beer hall,
founded in 1466, is friendly,
bustling and noisy. Excellent
Budvar beer washes down a
succession of classic Czech
dishes, including garlic soup,
pork with cabbage and
dumplings and the ubiquitous
fried cheese.

Nové Město

Albio

Truhlářská 20; tel: 222 325 414;
Mon–Sat 11am–10pm; €–€€;
metro: Náměstí Republiky; map
p.134 C2
Excellent vegetarian restaurant serving tasty and inven-
tive dishes, many cooked
with organic ingredients. The
menu (printed on recycled
cardboard) gives lots of
nutritional information, and
the dishes range from salad
with grilled goat's cheese

Left: Nostress café and
restaurant is also a photography gallery.

Vinárna

Traditionally, a *vinárna* was an
establishment serving wine
rather than beer, often from a
particular region or even vineyard. Nowadays is just another
term for a restaurant with some
pretensions to refinement.

---

and walnut oil to tasty noodle dishes. The ginger beer
is definitely worth a try, as
are the unpasteurised
Bernard dark and light ales.
The same owners run a well-
stocked organic supermar-
ket next door.

Cicala

Žitna 43; tel: 222 210 375;
Mon–Sat 11.30am–10.30pm; €€;
metro: Muzeum; map p.136 B1
Set in a basement off a busy
street, Cicala serves the most
authentic, and some of the
tastiest, Italian food in the
city. The menu offers a range
of antipasti, pasta and meat
dishes, in addition to the
daily specials.

Lahůdky Zlatý Kříž

Jungmannova 34; tel: 221 191
801; Mon–Fri 6.30am–7pm, Sat
9am–3pm; €; metro: Můstek;
map p.134 B4

Don't get ripped off at the
tourist restaurants on
Wenceslas Square. Instead,
follow the stream of ordinary
Czechs a few paces from the
square to this nondescript
shop on a side street. Inside,
behold a delicatessen classic. Jolly, motherly types
serve you from behind refrig-
erated counters rammed full
of typical Czech snack food
– *chlebíčky*. A slice of white
bread is loaded up with ham
or salami or maybe smoked
salmon, with a dollop or two
of cream cheese or potato
salad on top, and maybe a
gherkin garnish or a little
caviar. Order a side of
coleslaw or aubergine salad.
And take advantage of the
beer on tap. Then eat and
drink standing up at one of
the metal counters, or repair
to the garden around the
corner. And all very cheap
indeed.

Pivovarský dům

Ječná/Lípová 15; tel: 296 216
666; www.gastroinfo.cz/
pivodum; daily 11am–11.30pm;
€€; tram: 4, 6, 10, 16, 22, 23,
metro: Karlovo Náměstí; map
p.136 B2

Children
Prague restaurants are gradually becoming more attuned to the needs of visitors with young children, and some restaurants now have non-smoking sections, provide high-chairs and offer children's menus. Child-friendly establishments include Pizzeria Rugantino *(see p.116)*, Pizzeria Grosseto *(see p.119)*, and others, such as Taverna Olympos *(see p.119)*, with seating outside.

This microbrewery and restaurant is noted for its wide and varied range of beers brewed on the premises (even including coffee and banana beer). The hearty Czech food (such as roast pork and stuffed dumplings) is tasty and helps to soak up the drink. Among the other offerings are a wheat beer, mead and a delicious dark beer.

Taj Mahal
Škrétova 10; tel: 224 225 566; www.tajmahal.cz; Mon–Fri noon–11pm, Sat–Sun 1–11.30pm; €€; metro: Muzeum; map p.137 C1
Indian restaurant dishing up all the usual favourites, from chicken tikka masala to lamb korma and alu gobi to mattar panir, as well as naan, paratha and kulfi.

U fleků
Křemencova 11; tel: 224 934 019; www.ufleku.cz; daily 9am–11pm; €€; metro: Karlovo Náměstí; map p.136 A1
An ancient and well-known brewery with an illustrious past. Its present is not so admirable, filled as it is with hordes of tourists who bash tables, scoff down the goulash and quaff beer. However, the dark beer, brewed on site, is just as wonderful as ever. Avoid the 'free' Becherovka.

U Pinkasů
Jungmannova 16; tel: 221 1111 150; www.upinkasu.cz; daily 11.30am–1am; €€; metro: Můstek; map p.134 B4
While the ground floor and basement of this traditional establishment are given over to serious drinkers of Plzeňský prazdroj (which has been on tap here since 1843), the more genteel upper floor is an attractive restaurant serving a range of authentic Bohemian dishes.

Universal
V Jirchářích 6; tel: 224 934 416; www.universalrestaurant.cz; Mon–Sat 11.30am–12.30am, Sun 11am–midnight; €€; tram: 6, 9, 17, 18, 21, 22, 23; map p.136 A1
A reasonably priced and comfortable French bistro serving good food. Once settled in the slick interior, you can choose from dishes such as salade niçoise, steaks, and some classic desserts. Recommended.

Left: caption caption caption.

Vyšehrad

James Cook
Oldřichova 14; tel: 224 936 652; Mon–Fri 11am–11pm, Sat–Sun noon–11pm; €€; tram: 7, 18, 24, 53, 55; map p.136 C4
Everything here is orientated around the theme of the great explorer James Cook. The décor is awash with nautical paraphernalia, and the menu features cuisine from the four corners of the world. Tasty kangaroo steaks and good range of vegetarian dishes.

Smíchov and the Southwest

Potrefená Husa Na Verandách
Nádražní 84; tel: 257 191 200; www.pivovary-staropramen.cz;

Approximate prices for an average two-course dinner with a glass of house wine per person, including service and tax:

€	under €15
€€	€15–25
€€€	€25–40
€€€€	over €40

Left: keeping spirits open at U fleků.

building, dating from the 1891 Exhibition, perched on the edge of the Letná Park escarpment, with a spectacular view over the city. The traditional Czech menu comprises trout, pike-perch, duck, pigeon and game dishes, as well as a good selection of Moravian wines.

Vinohrady and Žižkov

Pizzeria Grosseto

Francouzská 2/náměstí Míru; tel: 224 252 778; www.grosseto.cz; daily 11.30am–11pm; €–€€; tram: 4, 22, 23, 57, metro: Náměstí Míru; map p.137 D2

Popular with local residents and office workers, this friendly restaurant serves some of the best pizza in Prague (all freshly cooked in a wood-burning oven). If you enjoy this one you might want to look out for their branches in Dejvice (Jugoslávských partyzánů 8) and Průhonice (Květnové náměstí 11).

Restaurant Atelier

Na Kovárně 8; tel: 271 721 866; www.restaurantatelier.cz; Mon–Sat noon–midnight; €€–€€€; tram: 4, 22, 23, 57

Smart French restaurant situated just to the east of

Havlickovy sady. The cooking is of a high standard, and unusually for Prague, is free from gimmicks and offered at very reasonable prices. As well as a summer terrace for dining outside, there is an impressive list of French wines.

Restaurant Myslivna

Jagellonská 21; tel: 222 723 252; daily 11am–11pm; €€; tram: 11, metro: Jiřího z Poděbrad

Located not far from the TV Tower, this restaurant is decked out with hunting trophies and, specialising in game, is intended for the dedicated carnivore. If it is furry and lives in the Bohemian forest there is a good chance you can eat it here. The wild boar and venison – all manner of body parts cooked in various ways with various sauces – are particularly recommended.

Taverna Olympos

Kubelíkova 9; tel: 222 722 239; www.taverna-olympos.eu; Mon–Sun 11.30am–midnight; €; tram: 5, 9, 26, 55, metro: Jiřího z Poděbrad; map p.135 E4

Cheerful and extremely popular Greek establishment, with a garden section that is popular with families. Greek wine as well as the usual range of tasty Hellenic comestibles.

Mon–Sat 11am–midnight; €; tram: 6, 9, 12, 20, 58; metro: Anděl

The Staropramen brewery's smart bar-restaurant offers 10 varieties of their beer alongside traditional high-carb Czech food to soak up the alcohol. Good value for money.

SEE ALSO FOOD AND DRINK, P.60

Holešovice

La Crêperie

Janocského 4; tel: 220 878 040; Mon–Sat 9am–11pm, Sun until 10pm; €€; metro: Vltavska

Although situated in a basement in Prague, this cosy restaurant has French owners, and serves authentic crêpes washed down with Breton cider.

Břevnov

Hanavský Pavilón

Letenské sady 6; tel: 233 323 641; www.hanavskypavilon.cz; daily 11am–1am; €€€; tram: 12

An eccentric neo-Baroque

Right: Staropramen, Prague's traditional favourite.

Shopping

Prague was never going to be on a par with London, Paris or New York for shopping, but even though the centre of Prague is now increasingly given over to shiny new shopping centres full of international high street chains, there are still some local shops worth searching out. For fashion, a sizeable number of international designers have set up shop along the posher avenues, and a number of Czech designers are beginning to make their mark. Service has also markedly improved, making the whole experience far more pleasant than in the early post-communist days.

Shopping Areas

Generally the best shopping is to be found in Staré and Nové Město, although some of the outlying districts now have huge shopping centres. The main commercial streets of central Prague with dependably long hours all year round are Václavské náměstí and Na Příkopě. If you are looking for expensive international fashion then head for Pařížská, which runs off Old Town Square.

Some of the small streets in the Old Town, such as V Kolkovně, Dušní, Týnská and Panská, have a number of exciting and unusual boutiques. The Týn Courtyard near the Old Town Square also has numerous little shops which are worth exploring, as do the back-streets of Malá Strana. If you are looking for a department store try either Kotva on náměstí Republiky or Tesco on Národní třída.

What to Buy

There are a number of locally produced items which are worth looking out for. You will not be able to avoid

Bohemian glass and china, held in high esteem throughout the world due to their quality and fair price. New items from major manufacturers are still excellent (try **Moser** or, for more contemporary styles, **Arzenal**), but now it's almost impossible to find a good deal in antiques shops. Antique dealers have become wise to the foreign market for their wares and have altered their prices accordingly.

If you're looking for something typically Bohemian to take home as a gift a bottle of the herbal liqueur Becherovka or some Slivovice is a good idea. Fruity wines from Bohemia and Moravia will also be appreciated. Wooden toys and puppets make excellent gift items for children. These can be found in the city-wide chain of **Manufaktura** shops. As well as toys, they also sell ceramics, fabrics and beautifully painted eggs.

Street vendors – concentrated in Hradčany and on the Charles Bridge – sell handmade goods, such as

marionettes and costume jewellery, as well as items of dubious use and value, such as refrigerator magnets depicting famous Prague sights.

MUSIC

Classical music CDs, especially those of Czech music from Supraphon, are cheaper than in the UK or US. The performances, by superb Czech ensembles and musicians, are always good and often thrilling. Also look out for recordings by local jazz and experimental rock musicians. Since the demise of Supraphon's own store one of the best places to find classical and contemporary music is the large **Bontonland Megastore** in the basement of the Koruna Building on the corner of Wenceslas Square. A good range of classical CDs can also be found at Via Musica.

FASHION

Although Prague seems overwhelmed by inter-

Right: shoping in Staré Město.

Left: The Kubista design shop.

to look out for include **Tatiana Kovarikova**, **Helena Fejková** and **Ivana Follová**, each of which have their own boutiques in Prague. Perhaps surprisingly, the city is also good for buying hats, and there are two long-standing firms that produce wonderful creations, **Model Praha** and **Tonak**.

KUBISTA AND MODERNISTA

These two shops are not only two of the most chic design boutiques in Prague but also also offer some of the best and more unusual souvenirs of your visit. Both capitalise on Prague's extraordinary outpouring of cutting-edge design during the first half of the 20th century. The first, **Kubista** not surprisingly, concentrates on superb reproductions of Czech Cubist works, including ceramics and furniture, as well as selling a number of original pieces. Fittingly, it is located in the Cubist House of the Black Madonna. **Modernista**, by contrast, concentrates on slightly later works, with reproductions of pieces by Adolf Loos and Functionalist designers.

Most shops open 10am–6pm, although those in the centre, catering largely to the tourist trade, often remain open late almost year-round. On Saturdays shops outside the centre of Prague generally close at noon or 1pm; shops in the centre, especially the larger department stores, may retain weekday hours on Saturday and Sunday as well.

national chains and designers, local fashions by Prague designers can be found, and their clothes are often inter-esting and well made. In Malá Strana try **Pavla & Olga** for one-offs and unusual pieces made in the shop by Pavla and Olga Michálková. In the Old Town there are a number of interesting places. **Klára Nademlýnská's** sexy and fashionable clothes are worth a look, while **Le Bohême** has some interesting pieces by Renáta Vokáčová. One of the most exciting places is **Hard-de-Core**, set up by designers Josefina Bakošová and Petra Krčková. Other names

121

Shop Listings

The main branches are given for the shops listed below; check their websites for other branches.

BOHEMIAN CRAFTS
Manufaktura
Melantrichova 17; tel: 221 632 480; www.manufaktura.biz; daily 10am–8pm; metro: Staroměstská; map p.134 B3
This is the main branch of a chain of stores specialising in local crafts, including wooden toys, hand-dyed fabric, ceramics and beautifully painted eggs. The chain has 10 outlets in Prague, so you are unlikely to miss it.
SEE ALSO PAMPERING, P.107

BOOKSHOPS
Prague has a number of excellent bookshops where you can find novels by Czech authors and books on local history.
SEE ALSO LITERATURE AND THEATRE, P.75

CRYSTAL AND GLASS
There is a huge amount of glass and crystal on display throughout the city, not all of it of high quality. The shops below are, if not the cheapest, all reputable and have interesting designs. Almost all of these places will also deal with the care and shipping of your new items, for a fee.

Arzenal
Valentinská 11; tel: 224 814 099; www.arzenal.cz; daily 10am–midnight; metro: Staroměstská; map p.134 A3
Modern designs by Bořek Šípek, coupled with a decent Thai restaurant.

Erpet
Staroměstské náměstí 27; tel: 224 229 755; www.erpet.cz; daily 10am–11pm; metro: Staroměstská; map p.134 B3
A wide range of top-notch crystal from a variety of manufacturers.

Moser
Staroměstské náměstí 15; tel: 221 890 891; www.moser-glass.com; Mon–Fri 10am–8pm, Sat–Sun 10am–7pm; metro: Staroměstská; map p.134 B3
The elegantly appointed flagship store of some of the best, most expensive Czech glassware.

DEPARTMENT STORES
The department store with the largest selection of goods, including gifts, fabric, clothes, shoes, perfume, groceries, travel accessories, stationery, electrical goods and books, is:

Kotva
Náměstí Republiky 8; tel: 224 801 111; Mon–Fri 9am–8pm, Sat 10am–7pm, Sun 10am–6pm; metro: Náměstí Republiky; map p.134 C3

FASHION
Though you will find few international-label bargains, young Czech designers offer high quality for surprisingly reasonable prices.

Bat'a
Václavské náměstí 28; tel: 224 218 133; www.bata.cz; Mon–Fri 9am–9pm, Sat 9am–8pm, Sun 10am–8pm; metro: Můstek; map p.134 B4
Although not high-end fashion, you still might want to pay a visit to the flagship store of this famous Czech shoe firm. The styles generally follow high-street trends.

Boutique Klára Nademlýnská
Dlouhá 3; tel: 224 188 769; www.klaranademlynska.cz; Mon–Fri 10am–7pm, Sat 10am–6pm; metro: Náměstí Republiky; map p.134 B2
Eminently wearable day and evening clothes, often given an understated sexy twist.

Hard-de-Core
Senovážné náměstí 10; tel: 777 094 421; www.harddecore.cz; Mon–Fri 11am–7pm, Sat 11am–5pm; metro: Náměstí Republiky; map p.134 C3
The brainchild of inspired designers Josefina Bakošová and Petra Krčková, this is not just a fashion shop but an institution stocking jewellery, ceramics and other handmade designs not to be found anywhere else. The owners will also design your party decorations and are happy to teach you some of their skills.

Helena Fejková Fashion Gallery
Štěpánská 61; tel: 724 125 262; www.helenafejkova.cz; Mon–Fri 10am–7pm, Sat 10am–3pm; metro: Muzeum; map p.134 B4

Right: Kubista Shop.

Sometimes quirky but always beautifully cut clothes, a place to find something for a special occasion.

if... Ivana Follová
Vodičkova 36; tel: 296 236 497; www.ivanafollova.com; Mon–Sat 10.30am–7pm; metro: Můstek; map p.134 B4
Modern, exciting design from one of the city's most interesting fashion houses. This boutique also has accessories by other Czech designers.

Laly
Štupartská 3; tel: 234 767 779; www.laly.cz; daily 11am–8pm; metro: Náměstí Republiky; map p.134 B3
A lovely, small vintage clothes shop with a fascinating selection of pieces, a place for lucky browsing.

Le Bohême
Štupartská 7; tel: 224 837 379; www.leboheme.cz; Mon–Sat 10am–7pm; metro: Náměstí Republiky; map p.134 B3
Casual but classic pieces designed by Renáta Vokáčová, with lovely linen dresses on display during the summer, many pieces are made on-site.

Model Praha
Václavské náměstí 28; tel: 224 216 805; www.modelpraha.cz; Mon–Fri 9am–7pm, Sat 10am–6pm, Sun 10am–5pm; metro: Můstek; map p.134 B4
Hat designers for anything from fashion shoots to theatrical costumes.

Pavla & Olga
Vlašská 13; tel: 728 939 872; Mon–Fri 2–6pm; tram: 12, 20, 22, 23; map p.132 C2
Fashion one-offs in interesting and unusual designs, made on-site, by local talents Pavla and Olga Michálková.

Tatiana
Dušní 1; tel: 224 813 723; www.tatiana.cz; Mon–Fri 10am–7pm, Sat 11am–4pm; metro: Staroměstská; map p.134 B2
Great womenswear from Tatiana Kovarikova; elegant and classic lines that are flattering and easy to wear.

Tonak
Palác Koruna, Václavské náměstí 1; tel: 224 218 506; www.tonak.cz; daily 10am–8pm; metro: Můstek; map p.134 B4
The Czech Republic has some excellent milliners; as well as Model Praha *(above)*, there is Tonak, great for wedding hats and formal wear.

MODERNIST REPLICAS
Kubista
Dům u Černé Matky Boží, Ovocný trh 19; tel: 224 236 378; www.kubista.cz; Tue–Sun 10am–6pm; metro: Náměstí Republicky; map p.134 B3
Wonderful reproductions of Czech Cubist works, as well as some originals for sale.

Modernista
Celetná 12; tel: 224 241 300; www.modernista.cz; Mon–Sat 11am–7pm; metro: Náměstí Republicky; map p.134 B3
This store takes the concept further with works by Adolf Loos and Functionalist designers, as well as Cubist pieces.

SHOPPING CENTRES
Four of the best, and largest, shopping centres are:
Myslbek
Na Příkopě 19; tel: 224 239 550; www.myslbek.com; Mon–Fri 9am–8pm, Sat–Sun 11am–7pm; metro: Můstek; map p.134 B3
Nový Smíchov
Plzeňská 8; tel: 251 511 151; www.novysmichov.eu; daily 9am–9pm; metro: Anděl
Palác Flóra
Vinohradská 149; tel: 255 741 712; www.palacflora.cz; daily 8am–midnight; metro: Flóra
Slovanský Dům
Na Příkopě 22; tel: 221 451 400; www.slovanskydum. com; daily 10am–8pm; metro: Můstek; map p.134 B3

Sport

More assiciated with heavy meals, sweet dumplings and drinking beer than sport, Prague nonetheless does have some outlets for physical exercise apart from that required by the lifting of a glass or knife and fork. The Czech Republic has a good record in international football, and Prague itself has three professional teams that fans might be keen on seeing. Even more popular is ice hockey, and the city has two of the country's best teams. For those looking to participate, the best bet is swimming. As a plus, there are natural outdoor pools as well as indoor ones for swimming lengths.

Football

Football has a good history in the Czech Republic, with at least one of Prague's teams regularly appearing in the Champions League. The city has three clubs, Sparta Prague (usually the most successful), Slavia Prague (their great rivals) and the more working-class Viktoria Žižkov. All three play each other during the season and local derbies are generally quite exciting.

CLUBS

Sparta Prague
Milady Horákové 98; tel: 296 111 111; www.sparta.cz; metro: Hradčanská

This is the best-known of the Prague clubs outside of the Czech Republic as they often play abroad (they reached the semi-final of the Champions League in 1993). They were founded in 1893 and, along with Slavia Prague, tend to contribute most of the players to the Czech national team. They have won the Czech League eight times since 1989.

Slavia Prague
Zatopkova 2; tel: 233 081 753; www.slavia.cz; metro: Strašnická

The great rivals of Sparta Prague, Slavia are actually the older club, albeit by one year (it was founded in 1892). They play at the Eden ground (www.stadioneden.cz) from where they have had quite bit of success, particularly in Uefa competitions. A bit of trivia associated with the club is that they have been wearing the same colours (red and white) longer than any other club in the world.

Viktoria Žižkov
Seifertova Třída; tel: 221 423 427; www.fkvz.cz; metro: Florenc

Based in one of the more run-down bits of town, Viktoria have historically been in lower divisions than the other two main clubs. However, they still have a long history, being formed in 1903, and since the early 1990s have played in the first division and even won the Czech cup in 1994 and 2001.

Ice Hockey

Ice hockey is very popular in the Czech Republic, and

On the far (west) side of Petřín Hill from Malá Strana is the enormous **Strahov Stadium** (Velký Strahovský Stadión), built in the 1920s to designs by Alois Dryák. It was used by the Czech nationalist Sokol (or 'Falcon') movement for mass gymnastic displays. The movement's gatherings were later banned by the communist authorities because of the undesirable similarities to organisations in Nazi Germany and because of its propagation of nationalist aspirations. The Sokol movement has since, however, been reformed (see www.sokol-cos.cz for more information).

internationally the country has always done very well. Prague has two teams which attract an enthusiastic local following. Like the football teams, they are rivals and are named Sparta and Slavia.

CLUBS

HC Sparta
Tesla Arena, Za Elektrárnou 419; tel: 266 727 411;

Left: football rules in the Czech Republic.

This is the largest pool complex in the city, with two outdoor pools, one inside, diving boards and a waterslide.

OUTDOOR POOLS

There are five natural swimming pools in Prague, maintained by the Hygienická Stanice Hlavního Města Praha (www.hygpraha.cz); smiley, or other, faces on their website tell you when the water quality is good. Open for swimming during the summer (let's face it, you wouldn't want to face the sub-zero temperatures during winter), access is free and the water might be a bit green but is generally clean.

Koupaliště Džbán
Divoká Šárka; tram: 8
Koupaliště Hostivař
K Jezeru; bus: 232
Koupaliště Lhotka
Nad Koupadly; tel: 241 490 914; bus: 121
Koupaliště Šeberák
Kunratice; bus: 114
Rybník Motol
Ulice Zahradníčkova; tram: 4, 9, 10

www.hcsparta.cz; metro: Nádraží Holešovice

Like their namesakes of the football club, this ice hockey team was founded back in 1893. Sparta have a distinguished history and have long battled with their rivals Slavia for domination of the Czech hockey league.

HC Slavia
Vladivostocká 1460; tel: 267 311 417; www.hc-slavia.cz; metro: Strašnická

The second Prague team, Slavia play at the large O2 Arena (www.o2arena.cz). Founded back in 1900, they have a number of successes to their name, not least being the 2008 champions.

Swimming

There are a number of pools in Prague, ranging from Olympic-sized ones for swimming lengths to natural swimming holes in the parks.

Aquacentrum
Letňany Lagoon
Tupolevova 665; tel: 283 921 799;

www.letnanylagoon.cz; daily 6am–10pm; admission charge; bus: 140,186,195

A 25m (82ft) pool that has good safe areas for children, including a waterslide. There are also a couple of lanes set aside for more serious swimming.

Plavecký stadion Podolí
Podolská 74; tel: 241 433 952; www.pspodoli.cz; daily 6am–9.45pm; admission charge; tram: 3, 16

Right: but ice hockey is not far behind.

Transport

Prague is an extremely easy place both to reach and to travel around. There are many flights from elsewhere in Europe, and it is easy to reach by train. The city's public transport system is extremely efficient, and the level of service and integration is enough to make someone from the UK weep. Driving is not a good idea in Prague: the roads are already extremely busy and the parking restrictions and complicated one-way system should deter anyone thinking of hiring a car. Besides, with such a walkable city centre and the bus, tram and metro network a car is more of an irritation than a useful asset.

Arrival by Train

There are direct train connections to Prague from many places in Germany and Austria. From Munich the journey takes approximately 6 hours, from Frankfurt 7 hours, Berlin 4½ hours, Hamburg 7 hours and Vienna 4 hours. Most trains from southern Germany and Austria arrive at the Main Station (*Hlavní nádraží*). Trains from the west stop at Prague-Holešovice Station and many proceed on to the Main Station.

The most direct way to reach Prague from London by train is via Paris and Frankfurt, which takes around 18 hours (for details and booking check with www.raileurope.co.uk). Some of these trains arrive at Smíchov.

Arrival by Air

The national airline is **ČSA** (České Aeroline; www.csa.cz), and they and British Airways (www.ba.com) fly direct from the UK. Numerous budget airlines now fly to Prague. From the UK these include: **easyJet**, flying from Gatwick,

There are some unscrupulous taxi operators in Prague, and overcharging is a common complaint. Phoning a taxi is cheaper than hailing one, as rates are lower and you won't be overcharged. Two reputable firms with staff who speak English are AAA Taxi (tel: 140 14) and Profi Taxi (tel: 844 700 800).

Bristol, East Midlands, Newcastle and Stansted (www.easyjet.com); **BMIbaby** from Birmingham, Cardiff, East Midlands and Manchester (www.bmibaby.com); and **Jet2** from Belfast, Edinburgh, Leeds-Bradford and Manchester (www.jet2.com). The Czech-based **Smart Wings** flies from elsewhere in Europe (www.smartwings.net).

From North America the only airline to fly direct to Prague, from New York and Toronto, is ČSA. For visitors coming from other starting points in Canada or the US it might make more sense to fly direct to London and then connect with a flight on one of the carriers listed above.

TO/FROM THE AIRPORT

Prague's expanded, modernised Ruzyně airport lies about 20km (12 miles) northwest of the city (for flight information tel: 220 113 314 or check www.csl.cz).

The cheapest way into the city from the airport (or vice versa) is by city transport. There are public bus services to the metro at Dejvická (buses 119 and 254), probably the most useful for the majority of visitors, the metro at Zličín (bus 100), and the metro at Nové Butovice (buses 179 and 225). Tickets are available from either the DPP counter in the arrivals hall or from machines by the bus stop just outside the terminal building. If you arrive late at night a night bus (510) will take you to the tram stop at Divoká Šárka, where you can pick up the night tram (51) into town.

A private minibus shuttle service, Čedaz (tel: 220 114 296; www.cedaz.cz), operates between the airport and náměstí Republiky with a stop at Dejvická metro, every half-hour between 5.30am

Left: Ruzyně airport.

day pass Kč330; and a five-day pass Kč500.

BUSES AND TRAMS

Buses, which are clean and punctual, tend to provide a service out to the Prague suburbs rather than compete with trams in the city. There is a comprehensive network of 31 tram routes which connect both sides of the river. Each tram stop shows the tram number passing there and a timetable. Most city maps show the tram routes in addition to the location of the major attractions. All trams run from 4.30am–midnight, but a number of routes are also designated as night routes and operate a service 24 hours per day. Purchase your ticket before you travel and validate it as you enter unless you are transferring from another tram or metro within your allotted time.

THE METRO

The extremely efficient Prague metro opened in 1974 and provides a great service for visitors. There are three interlinked lines, and metro maps can be found at each station. Metro signs above ground feature a stylised M incorporated into an arrow pointing downwards. The metro operates from around 4.30am until midnight.

and 9.30pm. They also have a number of minibuses that will take you directly to your hotel for a fee. However, the rates are almost as high as by taxi.

Two taxi firms operate from the airport into town, Airport Cars and AAA. Both have desks at arrivals. Taxis are lined up outside the arrivals exit. Rates, however, are relatively high compared to the other options.

Public Transport

Prague has a comprehensive and well-integrated public-transport system (www.dpp.cz) that provides a cheap and efficient service. Tickets and passes can be used on all forms of transport. Each ticket has a time limit, and you pay more for a longer limit. The cheapest ticket costs Kč18 and allows either 20–30 minutes of travel with no transfer or five stops on the metro with no line change. A Kč26 ticket allows 75 minutes of travel and allows line change or

tram transfer within that time. Children aged six to 15 pay half price.

Tickets can be bought at metro stations (there are automatic ticket machines which give instructions in English and supply change) or news-stands and some shops. They must be validated in the small yellow machines you will see when you catch the tram or arrive at the metro.

Day tickets or longer passes are also available and are valid for unlimited travel on all forms of transport. They are valid from the date stamped on them and do not have to be validated for each journey. Prices are as follows: 24-hour pass Kč100; three-

Right: trams are quick and efficient.

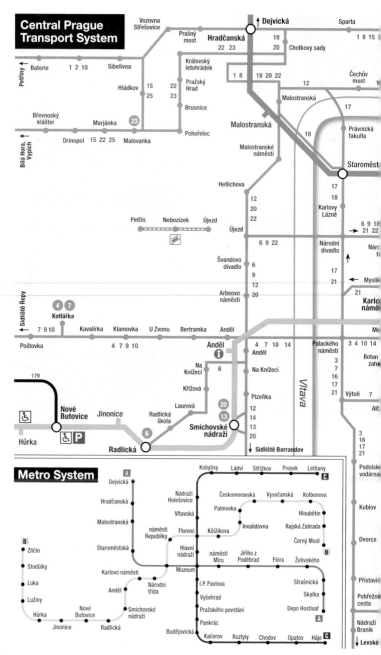

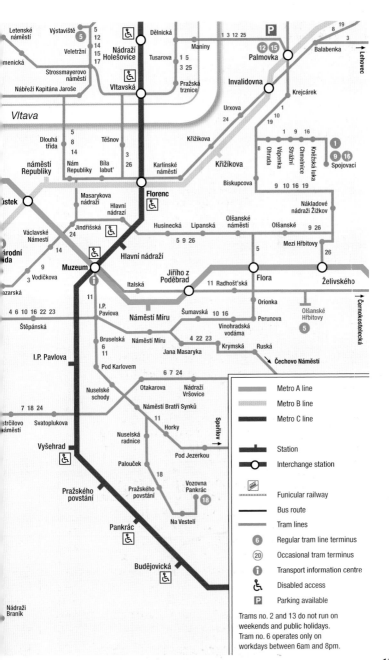

Atlas

The following streetplan of Prague makes it easy to find the attractions listed in our A–Z section. A selective index to streets and sights will help you find other locations throughout the city

Map Legend

≡	Motorway	▭▭	Railway
—	Dual carriageway	Ⓜ	Metro
	Main road	✉	Post office
	Minor road	🚌	Bus station
=	Footpath	✈	Airport
⊓⊓⊓	Steps	❶	Tourist information
	Pedestrian area	★	Sight of interest
	Notable building	✚	Cathedral/church
	Park	M̂	Museum/gallery
	Hotel	🎭	Theatre/concert hall
	Urban area	✡	Synagogue
	Non urban area	⚊	Statue/monument
† †	Cemetery	✚	Hospital

A **B** **C**

Na Ořechovce

Milady
Horákové

Strma

**Muzeum městské
hromadné dopravy**
(Public Transport Museum)

Patočkova

U Prašného mostu

p132 | p133 | p135

p136 | p137

Mariánské hradby

U Brusnice

Jeleni

KRÁLOVSKÁ
ZAHRADA

Míčovna
(Ball-Game Court)

Na Hubálce

Nad oktárnou

Jeleni

U Brusnice

Jízdárna
(Riding School)

U Prašného mostu

Kláš
sv.

1

U raka

HRADČANY

Národní
galerie/
Sternberský
palác

Obrazána
Pražského
hradu

Katédrála
sv. Víta

Nový Svět

sv. Jan
Nepomucký

Martinický
palác

Pražský
hrad

Tretí
nádvoří

Star
králov

Černínská

Na
náspu

Kapucínský
klášter

Loreta

Kanovnická

Arcibiskupský
palác

Hradčanské
nám.

Kapucínská

Toskánský
palác

Žám.
schody

Thun-
Hohenštej
palác

Keplerova

Černínský
palác

Narození
Páně

Schwarzenberský
palác

Ke hradu

Kajetán

sv.

Hlídkov

Za Hládkovem

Hládkov

Hládkov

Loretánské
nám.

Neruda

Savoy

Morstadtova

Domus
Henrici

Zlatá hvězda

Bretfeldský palác

Lichtenštejnský p

Parléřova

Úvoz

U červeného
lva

Janská

Kaiserštejn
p

2

Patočkova

Na
Panenské

Nad
Panenskou

Za Pohořelcem

Loretánská

U krále karla

Spořková

Bretislavova

Dům u velké boty

Vlašská

Myslbekova

Pohořelec

Questenberk

sv. Karel
Boromejský

Vlašská

Lobkovický
palác

Schönborns
pa

sv. Roch

**Strahovský
klášter**

Dlabačov

Památník nár. písemnictví

Vlašská

SCHÖNBORNS
ZAHRADA

**LOBKOVICKÁ
ZAHRADA**

Diskařská

Vaníčkova

STRAHOVSKÁ
ZAHRADA

Strahovská

MALÁ STRANA

Strahovskýs tunel

Chodecká

Diskařská

Malý
sportovní
stadión

Hladová zeď (Hunger Wall)

Strahovská

rozhledna
(Observation Tower)

Zrcadlová
Bludiště
(Mirror Maze)

SEMINÁŘSKÁ ZAHRADA

sv.
Vavřinec

F. Laub

3

Strahov

Olympijská

Petřín
(Petrin Hill)

Lanová dráha (Funicular Rai

V. Novák

K.H. Mácha

Diskařská

Stadión
Evžena
Rošického

Velký
Strahovský
stadión

Chaloupeckého

Štefánikova hvězdá
(Stefanik Observatory)

Stadión
přátelství

Vaníčkova

Jezdecká

KINSKÉHO ZAHRADA

Šermířská

Atletická

Šermířská

Vytlídková cesta

sv. Michal

4

Pod stadióny

letohrádek
Kinských
(Villa Kinský)

Hana
Kvapílová

0   400 m

Na Hřebenkách

Hoješkova

0   400 yards

ZŠ pro sluchově
postižené

A **B**

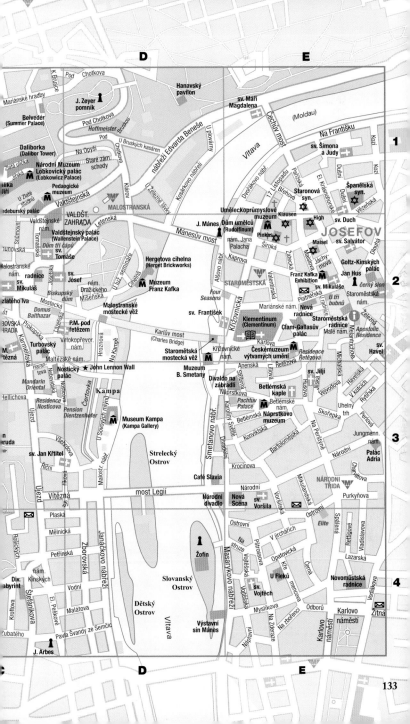

Mariánské hradby

J. Zeyer pomník

Hanavský pavilón

sv. Máří Magdalena

(Moldau)

Na Františku

Belvedér (Summer Palace)

Pod Chotkova

Hoffmeister

U plovárny

Na Frantíšku

Kozí

Daliborka (Dalibor Tower)

Pod Chotkova

Staré zám. schody

Vltava

Čechův most

sv. Šimona a Judy

Zlatá ulička

Národní Muzeum Lobkovický palác (Lobkowicz Palace)

Na Opyši

17. listopadu

Staronová syn.

Dvořákovo nábř.

sv. Duch

Dušní

Kozí

Pedagogické muzeum

Valdštejnská

MALOSTRANSKÁ

U plovárny

Španělská syn.

Věžeňská

deburský palác

VALDŠT. ZAHRADA

Letenská

Uměleckoprůmyslové muzeum

Klausen

High

sv. Duch

Valdštejnské nám.

Valdštejnský palác (Wallenstein Palace)

J. Mánes

Dům umělců (Rudolfinum)

Pinkas

Maisel

sv. Salvátor

JOSEFOV

Dům tří čápů

sv. Tomáše

Mánesův most

nám. Jana Palacha

Široká

Jáchymova

Maiselova

Goltz-Kinských palác

Malostranské nám.

Hergetova cihelna (Herget Brickworks)

Kaprova

Franz Kafka Exhibition

Jan Hus

černý šion

sv. Mikuláš

Biskupský dům

nám. Dražického

Muzeum Franz Kafka

Staroměstská nám.

Domus Balthazar

Malostranské mostecké věž

Four Seasons

STAROMĚSTSKÁ

Valentinská

sv. Mikuláše

Platnéřská

U tří bubnů

Apostolic Residence

zlatého lva

sv. František

Mariánské nám.

Nová radnice

Staroměstská radnice

Malé nám.

Melantrichova

sv. Havel

Turbovský palác

Biskupský dům

Křižovnická

Klementinum (Clementinum)

Clam-Gallasův palác

Apostolic Residence

Maltézská nám.

Karlův most (Charles Bridge)

Křižovnické nám.

Karlova

Residence Retězová

Mandarin Oriental

Nostický palác

★ John Lennon Wall

Staroměstská mostecké věž

Muzeum B. Smetany

Českémuzeum výtvamých umění

Anenská

sv. Jiljí

sv. Havel

Kampa

Divadlo na zábradlí

Liliová

Husova

Vejvodova

V kotcích

Havelská

Residence Nosticova

Náprstkova

Betlémská kaple

Betlémské nám.

Skořepka

Pachtův Palace

Uhelný trh

Pension Dientzenhofer

Museum Kampa (Kampa Gallery)

U Sovových mlýnů

Náprstkovo muzeum

Konviktská

Bartolomějská

Na Perštýně

Jungmann. nám.

Národní

Palác Adria

sv. Jan Křtitel

Říční

Strelecký Ostrov

Smetanovo nábř.

Divadelní

Krocinova

Mikulandská

NÁRODNÍ TŘÍDA

Charvátova

Vítězná

most Legií

Café Slavia

Národní divadlo

Národní

Nová Scéna

sv. Voršila

Purkyňova

Plaská

Ostrovní

Spálená

Mělnická

Ostrovní

V jirchářích

Elite

Retigiová

Vladislavova

Petřínská

Žofín

Na struze

Opatovická

Křemencova

Lazarská

Div. labyrint

Šteříánkova

Vodní

Slovanský Ostrov

Masarykovo nábřeží

Voršilská

Černá

Novoměstská radnice

Kroftova

El. Peškové

Malátová

Dětský Ostrov

Vojtěšská

U Fleků

Na zbořenci

Karlovo náměstí

Žitná

Zubatého

Pavla Švandy ze Semčic

Vltava

Výstavní sin Mánes

sv. Vojtěch

Myslíkova

Na Zderaze

Odborů

Náplavní

J. Arbes

133

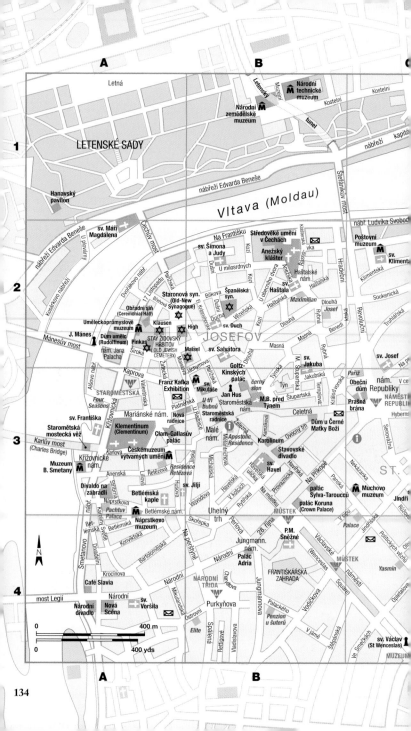

Letná

Letenský

Muzeum

Národní technické muzeum

Kostelní

Národní zemědělské muzeum

tunel

A **B** **C**

LETENSKÉ SADY

nábřeží Edvarda Beneše

Štefánikův most

nábřeží

kapit

1

Hanavský pavilon

náb. Ludvíka Svobod

Vltava (Moldau)

nábřeží Edvarda Beneše

sv. Máří Magdalena

Na Františku

Středověké umění v Čechách

Poštovní muzeum

Kozí

sv. Klimenta

sv. Šimona a Judy

Anežský klášter

vka

Bergšt

Klementská

náb. Kosárkovo nábřeží

Čechův most

U milosrdných

Dvořákovo náb.

17. listopadu

Pařížská

Břehová

Haštalské nám.

Dušní

Hradební

Soukenická

Na Františku

2

Staronová syn. (Old-New Synagogue)

Bílkova

Španělská syn.

U obecního dvora

Haštala

Maximilián

Dlouhá

Truhlářská

Revoluční

Obřadní síň (Ceremonial Hall)

Elišky Krásnohorské

Vězeňská

Kozí

Rybná

Josef

sv. Josef

Uměleckoprůmyslové muzeum

Klausen

Ducha

sv. Duch

Masná

Benedi

Mánesův most

J. Mánes

Dům umělc (Rudolfinum)

High

JOSEFOV

Pinkas

STARÝ ŽIDOVSKY HŘBITOV (OLD JEWISH CEMETERY)

Maisel

sv. Salvátora

Masná

sv. Jakuba

Rybná

Pařiž

nám. V ce

náměstí REPUBLI

nám. Jana Palacha

Široká

Masná

M. Štupartská

Obecní dům

Four Seasons

Kaprova

Valentinská

Franz Kafka Exhibition

Goltz-Kinských palác

Černý slon

Týn

Templová

Celetná

Stupartská

Prašná brána

Hybern

STAROMĚSTSKÁ

sv. Mikuláše

Jan Hus

M.B. před Týnem

Králodvor

sv. Františka

Křížovnická

Platnéřská

U tří bubnů

Staroměstská nám.

Dvořní tř

Dům u Černé Matky Boží

Senovážná

Staroměstská mostecká věž

Mariánské nám.

Nová radnice

Staroměstská radnice

Zelezná

Karolinum

3

Karlův most (Charles Bridge)

Klementinum (Clementinum)

Clam-Gallasův palác

Malé nám.

Melantrichova

Apostolic Residence

Stavovské divadlo

Nekázanka

ST.

Muzeum B. Smetany

Křížovnické nám.

Karlova

Českémuzeum výtvarných umění

Residence Retězová

Michalská

sv. Havel

Havelská

Na Příkopě

palác Sylva-Taroucců

Můchovo muzeum

Jindři

Anenská

Retězová

Husova

Rytířská

Na můstku

palác Koruna (Crown Palace)

Růžové

Divadlo na zábradlí

Betlémská kaple

sv. Jiljí

Veivodova

V kotcích

Provaznická

MŮSTEK

Palace

Pachtuv Palace

Náprstkova

Betlémské nám.

Skořepka

Perlová

28. října

Politických vězňů

Yasmin

Náprstkovo muzeum

Uhelný trh

Václavské

4

Smetanovo náb.

Divadlní

Konviktská

Na perštýně

Jungmann. nám.

P.M. Sněžné

MŮSTEK

náměstí

Café Slavia

Bartolomějská

Národní

Palác Adria

FRANTIŠKÁŘSKÁ ZAHRADA

Vodičkova

Štěpánská

Opatovi

most Legií

Národní divadlo

Nová Scéna

Národní

sv. Voršila

Mikulandská

Purkyňova

Jungmannova

Palackého

Václavské náměstí

Squae)

sv. Václav (St Wenceslas)

Krocínova

Ostrovní

Spálena

Vladislavova

V Jámě

V jámě

Štěpánská

Smečkách

MUZEUM

Elite

Penzion u šuterů

0   400 m
0   400 yds

N

A **B**

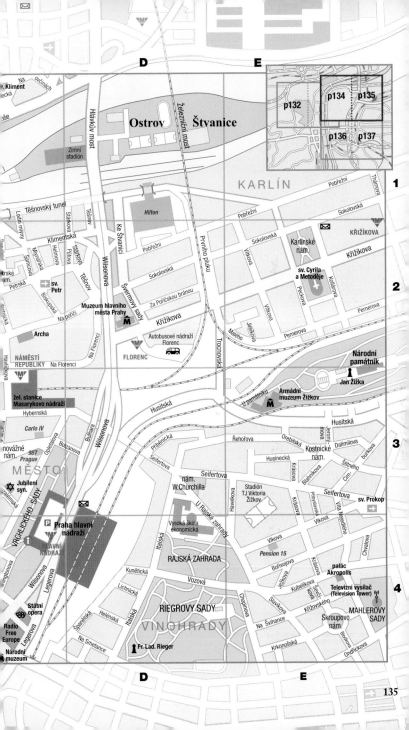

Ostrov Štvanice

Zimní stadión

p132   p134   p135

p136   p137

KARLÍN

Pobřežní

Thámova

Sokolovská

1

Na ovčínách

k. Kliment

ecká

še

Hlávkův most

Železniční most

Těšnovský tunel

Loďní mlýny

Klimentská

Myslíkova

Helmova

Samcova

Petská

krské

nám.

Bískupská

Na poříčí

sv. Petr

Archa

Tešnov

Štítkova

Pítlova

Ke Štvanici

Wilsonova

Švermovy sady

Pobřežní

Sokolovská

Za Poříčskou bránou

Muzeum hlavního města Prahy

Křížíkova

Hilton

Sokolovská

Vítkova

Karlínské nám.

sv. Cyrila a Metoděje

Koralova

Pernerova

Vítkova

Jeskova

Peckova

Malého

Pernerova

KŘIŽÍKOVA

Křížíkova

2

Prvního pluku

Autobusové nádraží Florenc

FLORENC

NÁMĚSTÍ REPUBLIKY

Havlíčkova

Na Florenci

Na Florenci

žel. stanice Masarykovo nádraží

Hybernská

Carlo IV

novážé nám.

987

Prague

MĚSTO

Opletalova

Bolzanova

Buharna

Wilsonova

Trocnovská

Husitská

Husitská

U památníku

Armádní muzeum Žižkov

Národní památník

Jan Žižka

3

Jubilejní syn.

Praha hlavní nádraží

HLAVNÍ NÁDRAŽÍ

VRCHLICKÉHO SADY

kmingtonova

Wilsonova

Legerova

Seifertova

Přibenická

Seifertova

nám. W.Churchilla

U Rajské zahrady

Vysoká škola ekonomická

Italská

Kunětická

Lichnická

Řehořová

Husinecká

Havelíková

Krásová

Blahníkova

Orebítská

Stadión TJ Viktoria Žižkov

Krásová

Vlkova

Bořivojova

Jezkova

Seifertova

Jeronýmova

Kostnické nám.

Dalimílova

burkova

Štítného

Cim.

Přibyslavská

Víta Nejedlého

Chvalova

sv. Prokop

Seifertova

Vlkova

Pension 15

Kubelíkova

Seific. Kova

Krásová

palác Akropolis

Televizní vysílač (Television Tower)

4

Státní opera

Radio Free Europe

Národní muzeum

Wilsonova

Legerova

Špandelská

Helénská

Italská

Chopinova

Na Smetance

RIEGROVY SADY

VINOHRADY

Vozová

RAJSKÁ ZAHRADA

Slavíková

Na Švíhance

Krížíkovského

Křkonošská

Skroupovo nám.

Ondříčková

Bíškova

MAHLEROVY SADY

Fr. Lad. Rieger

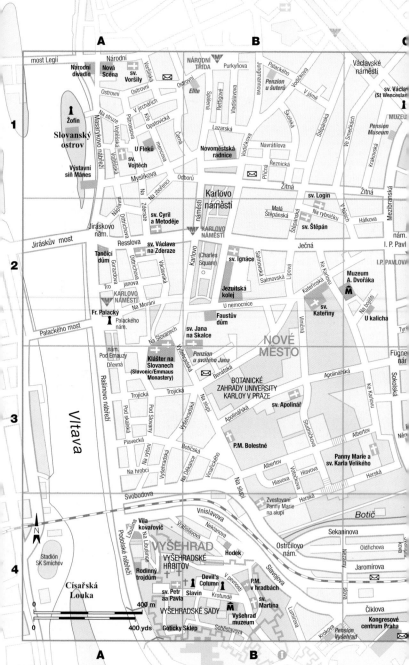

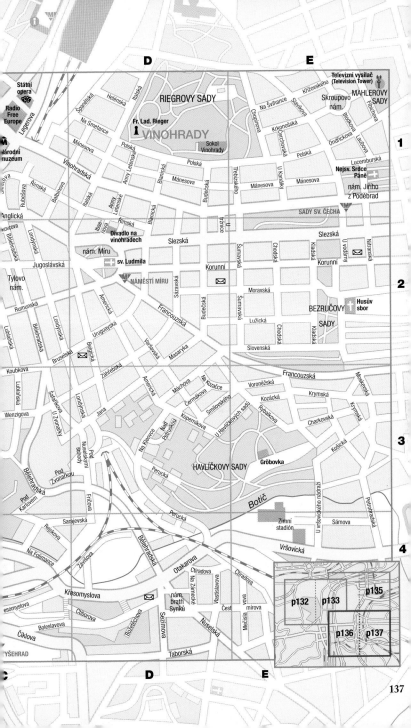

139

Index

Insight Smart Guide: Prague

Written by: **Maria Lord** and
Michael Macaroon

Edited by: **Jason Mitchell**

Proofread and indexed by: **Neil Titman**

All images © APA/ **Rod Purcell** except:

Alamy 40/41, 91B, 102/103, 119; **AKG
London** 95T; **APA/Glyn Genin** 5TR, 29B,
60, 112B; 112/113, 114, 117, 118; **Jon
Arnold** 28/29; **Axiom** 91T; **Bridgeman**
94/95; **Fotolia** 5TL; **Getty** 56B,
124/125, 125B; **Hotel Josef** 66; **Istock-
photo** 26B, 72/73, 73B; **Kobal** 52/53;
Laurent Philippe 56; **Leonardo** 68, 69;
Hynek Moravec 82B; **Mandarin Oriental** 65B; **Packa** 93TL/R; **ReflexStock**
90B, 92B; **Rudolphinium** 4T; **Scala**
95B; **Topfoto** 94T; **WpN** 58B

Picture Manager: **Steven Lawrence**

Maps: **Neal Jordan-Caws**

Series Editor: **Jason Mitchell**

First Edition 2009

© 2009 Apa Publications GmbH & Co. Verlag KG Singapore Branch, Singapore.

Printed in Singapore by Insight Print
Services (Pte) Ltd

Worldwide distribution enquiries:

Apa Publications GmbH & Co. Verlag KG
(Singapore Branch) 38 Joo Koon Road, Singapore 628990; tel: (65) 6865 1600; fax:
(65) 6861 6438

Distributed in the UK and Ireland by:

GeoCenter International Ltd

Meridian House, Churchill Way West, Bas-
ingstoke, Hampshire RG21 6YR;
tel: (44 1256) 817 987; fax: (44 1256) 817
988

Distributed in the United States by:

Langenscheidt Publishers, Inc.

36–36 33rd Street 4th Floor, Long Island
City, New York 11106; tel: (1 718) 784
0055; fax: (1 718) 784 0640l